FOLK TUNES
FROM THE WOMEN

FABER ff MUSIC

FOLK TUNES FROM THE WOMEN

Introduction

At the beginning of 2021, I received an email from a friend asking if I had any of my tunes written out. She was looking for female-composed material to teach to her fiddle group, having realised that everything on her 'possibles' list was written by men.

I immediately contacted a few of my female tune-writing friends to ask if they knew of any collections of tunes by women composers. They all said "no… but there absolutely should be such a thing." Some of them also suggested that in addition to a tune book, there should also be a website… and a series of podcasts… and we all got very excited.

So here it is! A tune book like no other! A book of contemporary folk tunes from 100 female composers based in Britain and Ireland, all from different areas, traditions and backgrounds. Some are successful professional musicians with lots of compositions to their name, others may have only written one tune. All of these composers answered my call to submit material for this *Folk Tunes from the Women* book. We all felt passionately that there was a real need for the book to exist, not only to make our own tunes more visible and accessible, but also to make it easier to learn and champion tunes from other women tune-writers.

This book is a collaborative, co-operative effort. All profits will be pooled and used to set up an ongoing resource to promote female folk composers. I am very grateful to the 'Tunebook Team' of extraordinary women, from different musical traditions, who played through the hundreds of submissions on their various instruments and helped to whittle the amazingly, gratifyingly (and dauntingly) huge number of tunes down to those you now have in your hands.

Although this material is presented collectively, I hope you will get a sense of the individuals involved and the processes and motivations behind our music. Some of these tunes were written in the darkest depths of grief, others are expressions of pure joy. There are stress-relievers, protests, distractions, memorials and meditations. Many tunes were written in gratitude - for life, for health, for friends and family. Some are professional commissions, others were given freely as gifts. Some are for dancing, some for listening. They are for births, deaths and everything between and beyond.

Notes on how to use this book:

Chords

To make the book a more useful tool for teachers and players we wanted as many tunes as possible to have chords to go with them. Some were submitted by the composers and there are a wide range of approaches, ranging from the simplest options to sophisticated chord progressions. Others were added by the 'Tunebook Team', who opted for fairly straightforward chords that should work on a variety of instruments. But these are just a suggestion. Feel free to experiment with your own chord choices! Where the composer feels strongly about the chords, or where the chords suit a particular instrument, we have tried to make this clear.

- Chords in brackets can be missed out if you prefer a simpler arrangement.

- Where there are two chords written e.g. C/E the first is the chord choice, and the second is the bass note (so this would be a C major chord, with an E at the bottom).

- If you see a chord that looks more complicated (e.g. suspended ('sus') chords or where the composer has added extensions such as 'add9' or similar) these extended notes have most likely come from the melodic shape of the tune. Some folk instruments, like melodeons and accordions, do not have all these chord options, in which case just play the basic chord.

- We have tended to write chords only when the harmony changes, so feel free to reiterate each chord as frequently as you wish until you see the next one.

Ornamentation

In traditional folk music, the ornamentation and grace notes play an important role in providing character and authenticity. In fact, some would say that it is in the ornamentation that the real art of traditional music lies. Folk music is inherently regional, and this is reflected in its ornamentation – we could devote an entire volume to the gracings of any one of the Irish counties alone! Our intention with this book however was to provide a varied selection of great tunes for you to explore. We are including ornamentation only where the composer herself has notated it. You may see ⅍ *mordent* or *tr* which indicates that the composer assumes you will do some sort of gracing here. Don't worry if you don't know what sort of gracing to use – just give it a try – we're happy that you want to play our tunes! And of course, if you do want to delve deeper then you could search up the composer and see if she has any recordings available or try listening to other musicians from the same tradition.

Tunebook Team notes
Occasionally, in addition to the text provided by the composer herself, one of the Tunebook Team (TT) has added an extra comment or suggestion.

Thanks to:
The Tunebook Team: Jo Freya, Mairearad Green, Amy Thatcher, Corrina Hewat, Angharad Jenkins, Anna Massie and Rebecca McCarthy-Kent.
Rachael McShane, for sending the email that started this whole thing off.
Simon Thoumire at Hands Up For Trad.
Real World Works
Everyone who submitted tunes – thank you so much for your interest and your support, and for trusting us with your music.

Now, you have the book. Explore the music. Enjoy it. Play the tunes, share the tunes, teach the tunes... and WRITE MORE!

Kathryn Tickell

© 2023 by Faber Music Ltd
First published in 2023 by Faber Music Ltd
Brownlow Yard, 12 Roger Street, London WC1N 2JU
Cover design & illustration by Jesse Eve Watkins
www.jessicaevewatkins.com
Inside design by Liz Ogden
Edited for Faber Music by Lucy Holliday
Printed and bound in the UK by Caligraving Ltd
All rights reserved

ISBN10: 0-571-54287-5
EAN13: 978-0-571-54287-1

To buy Faber Music publications or to find out about the full range of titles available please contact your local retailer or Faber Music sales enquiries:

Faber Music Limited, Burnt Mill, Elizabeth Way, Harlow, CM20 2HX, England
Tel: +44 (0) 1279 82 89 82
fabermusic.com

CONTENTS

Jigs

Andy's Saltire 10	Amy Geddes
Anne et Ludovic 11	Sarah Northcott
Bealaclare Bridge 10	Mairéad Carey
The Caledon Line 12	Zoë Conway
Cannabeenie 11	Chloë Bryce
Chin Up 13	Rachel Cross
Don't Work Too Hard 14	Laura-Beth Salter
Dram Behind the Curtain 14	Mairearad Green
The East Clare Jig 15	Cli Donnellan
Flame 16	Bryony Griffith
Freya Dances 15	Mary Macmaster
George Veness 2 16	Jo Freya
Hunter's Path 17	Alison Jones
Jamie's Jig 17	Patsy Seddon
Jiggin' in Meitheal 18	Ernestine Healy
Kilmartin Glen Campsite 18	Rona Wilkie
Longshaw's 19	Alison Rowley
Maddie's Mayhem 19	Sophy Ball
Maisie's Jig 20	Kerry Russell
Michael's Birthday Jig 20	Margaret Robertson
Moniaive Jig 21	Wendy Stewart
Nuala Iona's Jig 21	Anna-Wendy Stevenson
The Sliding Rocks 22	Breesha Maddrell
Time for a Jig 22	Pam Bishop
Traeth y Bermo 23	Mirain Owen
Trip to Bucharest 24	Rachael McShane

9/8 & 12/8 jigs

A Quiet Autumn 26	Sarah Allen
Better Than a Bill 26	Anna Massie
Knoydart Ahoy! 27	Olivia Ross
Mirain 28	Helina Rees
Rede River Girls 27	Kathryn Tickell
Rhubarb and Ginger 28	Niamh Ní Charra
Seren yn y Glascoed 29	Angharad Jones
Springa Like Marit 29	Patsy Reid
Swerving for Bunnies 30	Ailie Robertson
Tilly Trip 30	Breesha Maddrell

Hornpipes

100 Days 33	Anna Massie
The Beachcomber 32	Kerry Russell
The Devil's Schottis 32	Vicki Swan
Jolly Roger 33	Pam Bishop
Mynydd Du 34	Lucy Rivers
Neuketyneuks 34	Fiona Driver
Tweedmouth Hornpipe 35	Susie Cochrane
Uncle Alan's Curtsy 35	Marina Dodgson
View from the Dam 36	Adèle Commins

Reels

Against Time *38*	Éadaoin Ní Mhaicín
Angus Grant Sings the Grateful Dead *38*	Sarah McFadyen
Back Home in Önsbacken *39*	Karen Tweed
Cissy Middleton of Gawthrop *40*	Carolyn Francis
Da Fiddler Fae Soothower *39*	Margaret Robertson
Dusseldram *41*	Cathy Geldard
Fàilte *41*	Anna-Wendy Stevenson
The First Rule of Box Club *42*	Mairearad Green
Four for a Boy *42*	Alison Jones
Gen-Z *43*	Imogen Bose-Ward
Granny in the Attic *43*	Sarah Allen
Grey Days *44*	Chloë Bryce
Holtwood Reel *45*	Jess Arrowsmith
Johnnie Armstrong *44*	Patsy Seddon
Lady Isabella *45*	Lauren MacColl
Laidback Liz *46*	Eilidh Steel
Linda's Lilt *46*	Margaret Robertson
Never Trust Google Maps *47*	Isla Ratcliff
New Year's Resolutions *47*	Mairéad Carey
Parmogeddon *48*	Grace Smith
The Pinnacle *48*	Christine Edwards
The Port Dash *49*	Róisín Ward Morrow
The Red Crow *49*	Mairéad Ní Mhaonaigh
Thugainn *50*	Patsy Reid
Tripod's Frolics *50*	Tina Jordan Rees
The Underwater Gardener *51*	Sarah Northcott
The Welcome Home *51*	Kathryn Tickell
Y Selar *52*	Angharad Jenkins

Marches

A Far Away Rebel *54*	Adèle Commins
A Tune for Jean *54*	Lauren MacColl
Alan Friendly *55*	Corrina Hewat
Arthur's Seat *55*	Anna-Wendy Stevenson
Beccy's Big day *56*	Olivia Ross
The Great Exodus *56*	Gráinne Brady
The Halsway Parade *57*	Vicki Swan
John MacDougall's March *57*	Amy Geddes
Paperwork Sucks *59*	Sophy Ball
Pipe Major Bobby Coghill of Wick *58*	Eilidh Steel
Sheila & Gordon's Golden Wedding March *59*	Marie Fielding
Society's Welcome to the Year '21 *60*	Claire Gullan

Polkas

The Ballymena Polka *62*	Ailie Robertson
Byddwch Yn Garedig *62*	Mari Morgan
Crow Road Croft *63*	Lauren MacColl
The Lockdown Polka *63*	Maeve McCann
Puck Goes Dancing *64*	Harriet Power

Season's Promise 64	Laurel Swift
The Shores of Loch Awe 65	Karen Woods
The Two-Part Pour Polka 65	Niamh Ní Charra
Up the Lum 66	Rachel Newton
Wilbur's Wonder 66	Sue Harris

Waltzes & Mazurkas

A Girl on the Rock 68	Kate Strudwick
A Tune for Lewis 68	Kirstie McLanaghan
Another Day 69	Karen Gledhill
Bert Mackenzie's 70th Birthday Waltz 70	Louise Mackenzie
Bresychen Ddiog 71	Elsa Davies
The Calm Between the Storms 69	Martha Woods
Castle Hill 70	Delyth Jenkins
The Christmas Eve Waltz 72	Marie Fielding
Elvaston Castle 71	Jess Arrowsmith
Key Workers Waltz 73	Angharad Jenkins
Leaving Whitby 73	Helen Bell
Lurand 74	Heather Woodbridge
Maggie West's Waltz 74	Mairearad Green
Mazurka 75	Catrin Ashton
Mazurka in the Dark 76	Harriet Power
Mike & Catherine's 75	Isla Callister
Otis & Deanie 77	Sarah McFadyen
Pandemonium 76	Rebecca McCarthy-Kent
Rosa's Waltz 77	Delyth Jenkins
Steve Fisher's Lament 78	Mel Biggs
Swirling Flames 79	Jo Freya
Too Cute to Correct 79	Amy Thatcher
The Trip to Gorthleck 80	Mary Macmaster
Waltzing at Giggleswick 81	Rachael McShane

Crooked Tunes

Bonfire Night 84	Helen Gentile
Haul ar y Carreg 85	Stacey Blythe
The Joy of It! 86	Catriona Macdonald
La Femme du Saule 87	Sarah Northcott
Loch nan Claidheamhan 84	Rachel Newton
Mr Collins' No. 2 85	Jess Arrowsmith
Old Wax Jacket 88	Tamsin Elliott
The Phrayes 89	Corrina Hewat
Pillowfish 88	Helen Bell
The Rest and be Thankful 90	Marit Fält
Rounding Malin Head 90	Zoë Conway
Tha i air sràid 91	Rona Wilkie

Strange Times

Aye Fly 94	Bryony Griffith
Clogfaenydd 95	Bethan Rhiannon
The Dale 94	Grace Smith
Ducks at Luss 95	Tina Jordan Rees
Emergency of the Female Kind 96	Amy Thatcher

For Marie 96	Isla Callister
King Bramble 97	Laurel Swift
Last Trip to Dunbar 98	Catherine Robson
Paw Bran 98	Martha Woods
Yer Peaks Are Getting Peakier 97	Laura-Beth Salter

Miscellaneous

Akaroa 100	Annette Davies
Alaw i Nansi 101	Llio Rhydderch
The Bass Strathspey 101	Corrina Hewat
The Bird Man of Chambers Street 103	Eilidh Steel
Claggy Jacks 102	Margaret Watchorn
Dark Stacks 104	Inge Thomson
Dawns Elmo 103	Cerys Hafana
'Dolig Abertawe 105	Angharad Jenkins
The Eggshell Brewery 104	Rachel Newton
Good News for Pigs 105	Helen Gentile
Kingfisher on the Clun 106	Ruth Angell
Learn to Hambo! 106	Sophy Ball
The Lighthouse Lovers 107	Karen Tweed
Morag's Welcome 108	Claire Gullan
Revoke Article 50 107	Isla Ratcliff
Rothbury Road 109	Kathryn Tickell
Sandy MacDonald of Skye 109	Gráinne Brady
Spring At last 110	Martha Woods
Tanteeka 110	Jo Freya
Tune for A.Lien 111	Catriona Macdonald
Welcome Joy and Welcome Sorrow 112	Jane Harbour

Airs

A Tune for Frankie 115	Mairéad Ní Mhaonaigh
April's Child 114	Amy Thatcher
Bright Field 114	Rowan Rheingans
Deoraíocht an t-Saighdiúra 115	Niamh Ní Charra
Don MacDonald 116	Sue Harris
I Fear You Just as I Fear Ghosts 116	Jane Harbour
Ivan's 117	Ailie Robertson
Lament for Emily Davison 118	Susie Cochrane
The Legacy 118	Cli Donnellan
Lle Arall 119	Kate Strudwick
Llidiart y mynydd 119	Gwen Màiri
Mae'r Gaeaf yn Dyfod 121	Branwen Mai Roberts
Marram 120	Margaret Watchorn
May the Road Rise Up to Meet You 121	Wendy Stewart
Rita Hunter of Aultbea 122	Valerie Bryan
Selkie's Echo 122	Alison Jones
Stretching Heart 123	Christine Edwards
Suilven 124	Fiona Driver

*All the women featured in this book have donated their royalties
to set up a website and resources to promote women tune writers.
This is being managed by the Scottish traditional music education charity, Hands Up For Trad.
Follow our progress here: tunesfromthewomen.co.uk*

Jigs

*I love a good jig… and there are some great examples here!
In Northumberland we tend to play jigs with a real swing
to them, almost a dotted rhythm. Some of these tunes suit that
way of playing, some want to be played in a more flowing and
sinuous manner, some want to be played fast and others want you
to slow right down. There are so many different regional variations
and terminologies – single jigs, double jigs, slides, slipjigs etc.
that we decided to simplify things and keep all the 6/8 jigs here
and put the 9/8s and 12/8s together in their own category.*

Kathryn Tickell

ANDY'S SALTIRE
Composed by Amy Geddes

'Andy's Saltire' was written on 12th September 1997, the day after Scotland voted yes to devolution and the creation of a Scottish Parliament. On referendum day, my dad proudly flew his saltire from the garden gate. We woke up the next day to find it gone. The thieves have never been apprehended – the case remains open – but my Dad got a celebratory jig and a parliament, more than making up for the loss!

BEALACLARE BRIDGE
Composed by Mairéad Carey

This double jig is one of the first tunes I ever composed, and is named after a picturesque spot in the parish of Aughadown in West Cork.

ANNE ET LUDOVIC
Composed by Sarah Northcott

This jig was written to celebrate the marriage of my good friend and wonderful Breton harpist Anne Postic to Ludo Reungoat in 2009. I first met Anne and her lovely family on an exchange organised by Edinburgh's Adult Learning Project in 1998.

CANNABEENIE
Composed by Chloë Bryce

Ceannabeinne beach is situated on the far north coast of the Scottish mainland. I have fond childhood memories of summers spent on this beach. 'Cannabeenie' is how my dad pronounces the Gaelic name, meaning 'the end of the mountains'.

THE CALEDON LINE

Composed by Zoë Conway

A very traditional sounding, 3-part melodic jig named after an old trainline
near my mother's home in Middletown, Co. Armagh.

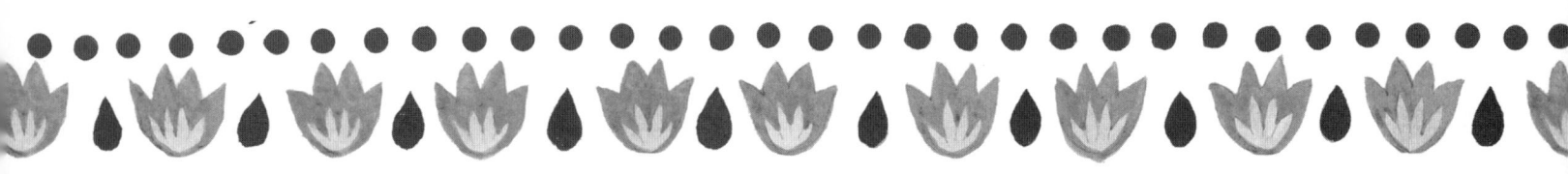

CHIN UP

Composed by Rachel Cross

I wrote this tune when I was feeling a bit down and it may have helped to cheer me up.
Hopefully it will help cheer up someone else having a low day!

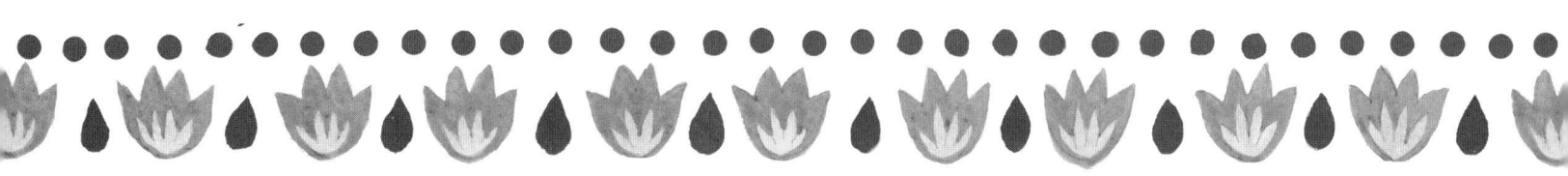

DON'T WORK TOO HARD

Composed by Laura-Beth Salter

This upbeat jig was written after the first time I had tunes with my Kinnaris Quintet pal, Aileen Reid.
We sat up all night playing, and then I foolishly tried to pretend to my taxi driver I was on my way to work at
6am instead of on my way home. He didn't buy it, laughing, "Don't work too hard" as I got out of the cab!

DRAM BEHIND THE CURTAIN

Composed by Mairearad Green

My Grandfather, Alisdair Macleod, sometimes kept a glass of whisky in the kitchen window.
This tune features on Eddi Reader's version of the Burns' song 'Comin' thru the Rye'.

THE EAST CLARE JIG
Composed by Cli Donnellan

A reflective tune, influenced by the landscape of my native East Clare.
The movement from the lower octave notes to the higher in the second part is akin to the
flowing water that is Lough Derg meeting the mountains of Tipperary across from my home.

FREYA DANCES
Composed by Mary Macmaster

'Freya Dances' was a birthday present.
N.B. the suggested accompanying notes with this tune are bass lines rather than chords.

FLAME

Composed by Bryony Griffith

Originally written in Bm and played slowly for Black Swan's 'Fire Dance' at Sidmouth 2003,
but it seems to get played much quicker in the more friendly key of E minor at sessions.

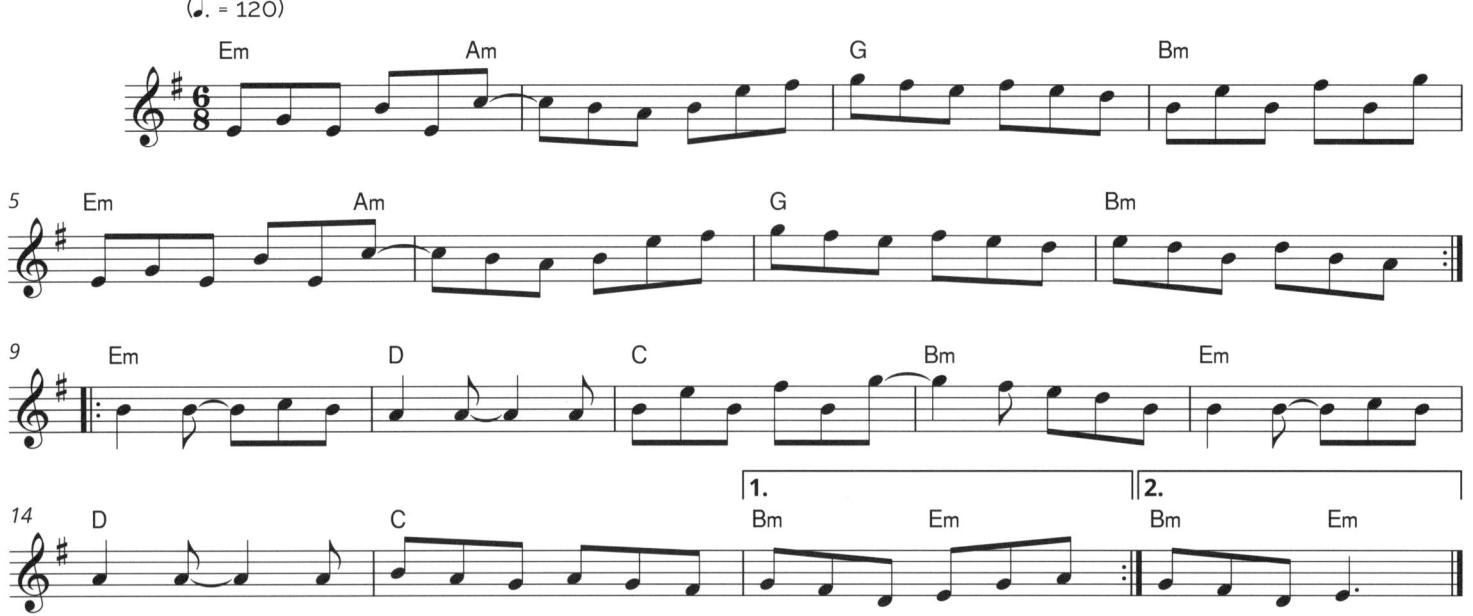

GEORGE VENESS 2

Composed by Jo Freya

This tune is dedicated to George Veness who was a regular participant in Halsway Summer Schools. He sadly died in early 2021. George had many health issues, but it never stopped him dancing. This quirky little jig was to reflect his joy and mischievous nature. On the one hand, like the 'A' music everything would seem normal and predictable but then, like the 'B' music, George never did quite what you expected. It has the number '2' because I wrote another tune for him at the same time which was a lament and is called 'George Veness 1' of course!

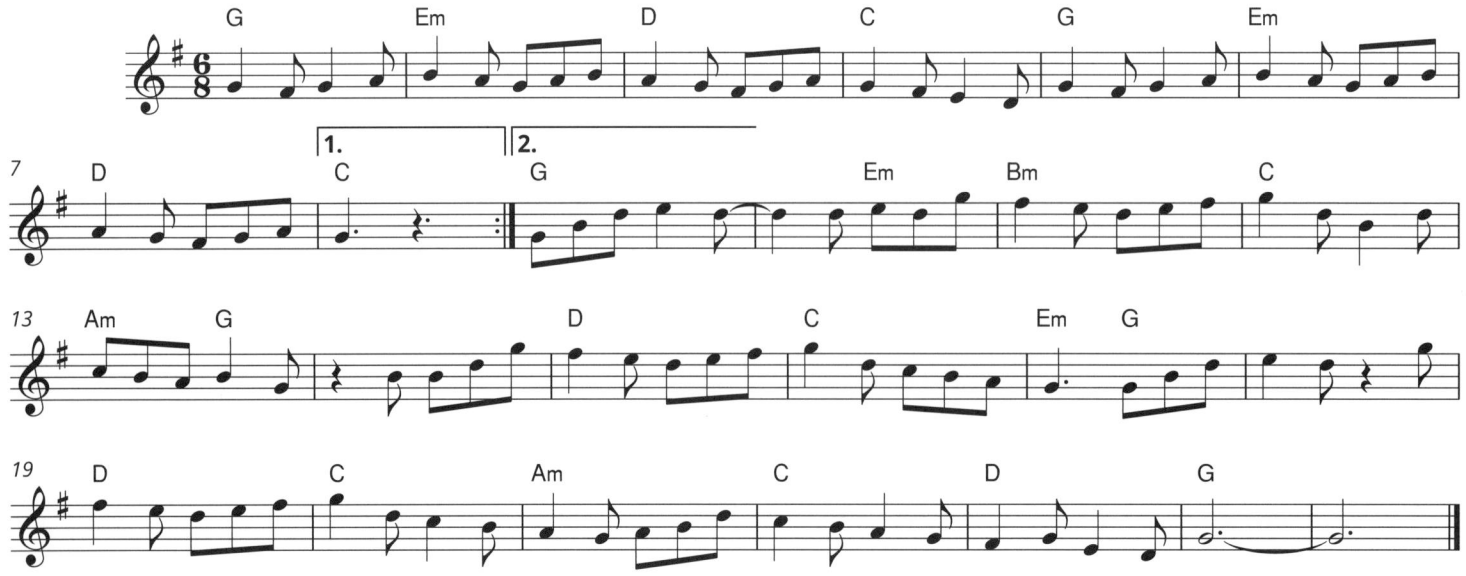

HUNTER'S PATH
Composed by Alison Jones

After a steep climb from Fingle Bridge, the Hunter's Path opens out onto incredible views over the River Teign and the lush valley below. This has become my special birthday walk with friends and family. It's a gentle jig.

JAMIE'S JIG
Composed by Patsy Seddon

This jig was written for my son Jamie Steele. His father was Davy Steele, the well-loved singer song-writer and guitarist, and Jamie shares his father's passion.

JIGGIN' IN MEITHEAL

Composed by Ernestine Healy

This tune is from a suite of music that was written for the orchestra from the Meitheal Summer School in 2016.

KILMARTIN GLEN CAMPSITE

Composed by Rona Wilkie

Written for a beautiful weekend where we camped in the middle of a stone circle in Kilmartin Glen, only to be told to leave by the farmer. This tune is written to reflect on the magic of the experience.

LONGSHAW'S
Composed by Alison Rowley

This jig was written after a beautiful day walking around the Peak District close to the National Trust's Longshaw Estate. I was proud of my adventurous hiking abilities and wrote this jaunty tune to celebrate!

MADDIE'S MAYHEM
Composed by Sophy Ball

This was written for my fiddle student Maddie Edgoose, a lovely player and all-round fabulous person. When she started heading to festivals with her friends, she managed to get into all kinds of mayhem.

MAISIE'S JIG

Composed by Kerry Russell

Written in memory of my Dublin ancestor Maisie Fitzpatrick, and the
convoluted tale of how I found the other half of my family.

MICHAEL'S BIRTHDAY JIG

Composed by Margaret Robertson

This tune was requested by a pupil for her dad's birthday and to cheer him up as he'd recently lost two close
family members. After such a lovely, thoughtful request from a teenage daughter, who could refuse her a tune!

MONIAIVE JIG
Composed by Wendy Stewart

Written originally to celebrate Andy Goldsworthy's Striding Arches, which sit around the
head of Glencairn, up Dalwhat Glen above the festival village of Moniaive. Expect the unexpected!
Resolve to a held E note and A chord if needed at the end.

NUALA IONA'S JIG
Composed by Anna-Wendy Stevenson

Written for my goddaughter.

THE SLIDING ROCKS
Composed by Breesha Maddrell

This tune was written after conversations with my grandmother, Doris Catherine McGain, who, as a child, used to delight in climbing up to the top of the rocks in the quarry just outside Cregneash in the south of the Isle of Man, only to slide down them again and again, much to the horror of her mother.

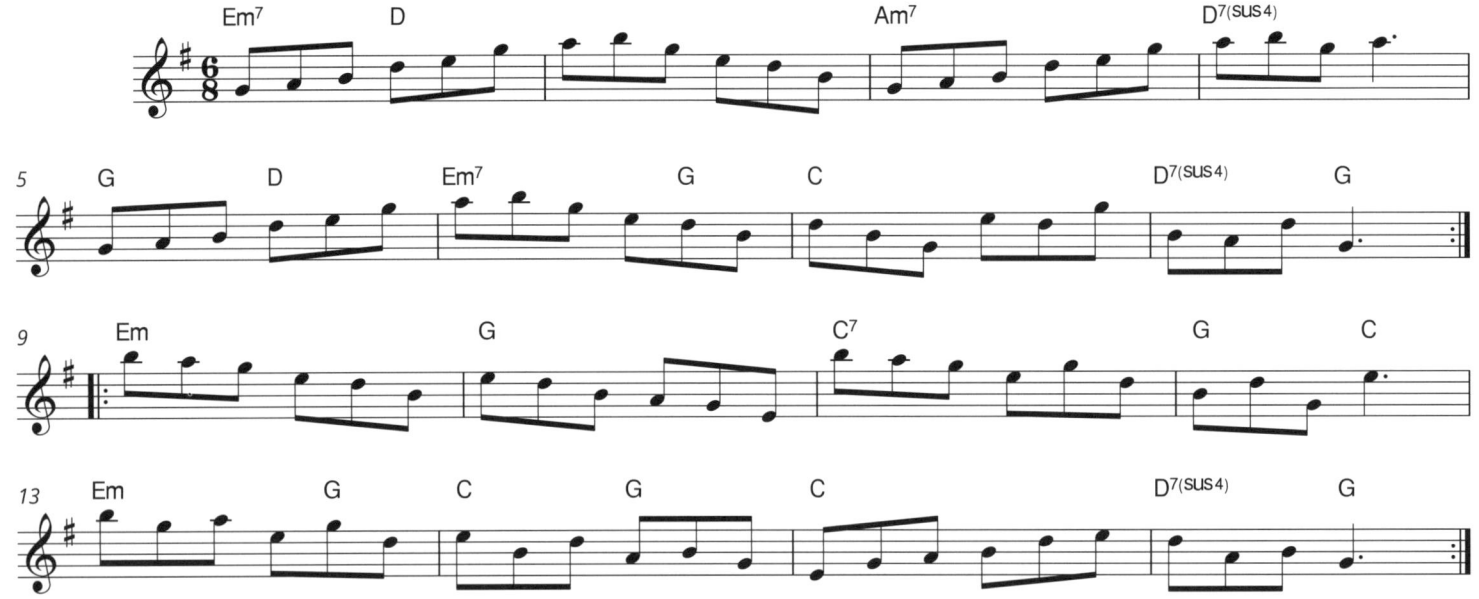

TIME FOR A JIG
Composed by Pam Bishop

'Time for a Jig' is a response to a friend reminding me I owed him a letter.

TRAETH Y BERMO

Composed by Mirain Owen

I wrote a tune over the lockdown that was longing for the beach I used to go to with my grandparents, it's called 'Traeth Y Bermo', which translates to 'The Beach of Barmouth'. Although I wrote this tune longing for the beach, it is a happy tune evoking memories of making sandcastles and jumping over waves! I hope you enjoy!

TRIP TO BUCHAREST

Composed by Rachael McShane

Written to 'commemorate' a hideous and ultimately futile journey from Romania to Bulgaria.
Landing at Heathrow, I discovered my cello had been wrecked on the flight.
It's an angry tune but was cathartic to write, and good fun to play. Recorded on *Matachin*, by Bellowhead.

9/8 & 12/8 Jigs

All the tunes in this section and the 'Jigs' section have their quavers grouped in threes, but where the jigs have a time signature of 6/8 and have two groups of three quavers to the bar, these tunes either have three groups of three (9/8) or four groups of three (12/8).

In Irish traditional music there are many different types of tune within these time signatures, including slipjigs, hop jigs, single jigs and slides. There have been long discussions about how to differentiate between all of these, but we decided that in this book we would just present you with the tunes themselves.

There are some lovely slipjigs in this section which would be perfect for Irish step dancing and lend themselves to being played in a more laid-back style, with a slower tempo than regular jigs and reels. You will also find tunes with a more contemporary approach, exploring syncopation and influences from further afield. We hope you enjoy exploring them.

Rebecca McCarthy-Kent

A QUIET AUTUMN

Composed by Sarah Allen

'A Quiet Autumn' was recorded on Flook's first studio album *Flatfish*.
I wrote it one Autumn that ended up being anything but quiet.

BETTER THAN A BILL

Composed by Anna Massie

I spent lockdown 2020 at home with my parents in Fortrose, on the Black Isle. During that time, folk started sending me letters, postcards and even the occasional bottle of gin... All much better than bills!

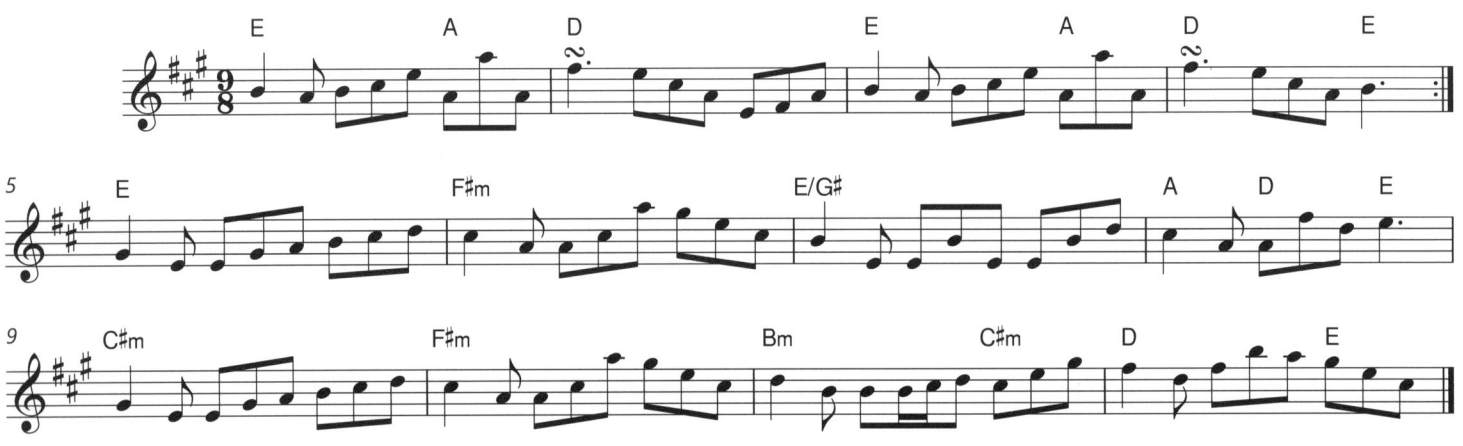

KNOYDART AHOY!
Composed by Olivia Ross

Each year around October time when I see an email come through titled Knoydart Ahoy I know there's a brilliant weekend of songs, tunes and side splitting laughter coming up very soon.

REDE RIVER GIRLS
Composed by Kathryn Tickell

Written for my daughter Casey and her friends Tuuli and Romy after a golden summer containing everything a child could want: friends, family, sun, sausages cooked over an open fire, a handy river to splash about in… and an inflatable unicorn.

MIRAIN

Composed by Helina Rees

This is named after my youngest daughter. Her quirky, unpredictable character inspired me to come up with
a tune full of joy and surprises! I'd expect this tune to be played exactly as written.
However, the chord sequences are optional.

RHUBARB AND GINGER

Composed by Niamh Ní Charra

This is a slip jig I wrote and named after my grandmother Olive's lovely jam!

SEREN YN Y GLASCOED
(STAR IN THE GREENWOOD)
Composed by Angharad Jones
A slip jig, because you can never have too many slip jigs!

SPRINGA LIKE MARIT
Composed by Patsy Reid

This tune was inspired by the 3/4 Polska feel that I learnt to play a lot with Marit Falt, who comes from Norway. I wanted to really get the 1 and 3 accented beats across. The title came a little from Ewan MacPherson who performed this with me on my album, *The Brightest Path*, as he thought it actually sounded like a type of tune called a 'Springa'.

SWERVING FOR BUNNIES

Composed by Ailie Robertson

This slip jig was written as an apology to my bandmates after an incident involving a family of rabbits and a roadside ditch… Happy to say that all the rabbits survived!

TILLY TRIP

Composed by Breesha Maddrell

'Tilly Trip' was one of the childhood nicknames for my sister, Aalish – this tune is for her.
(Originally published in *Kiaull yn Theay 3*, Manx Heritage Foundation, 2009).

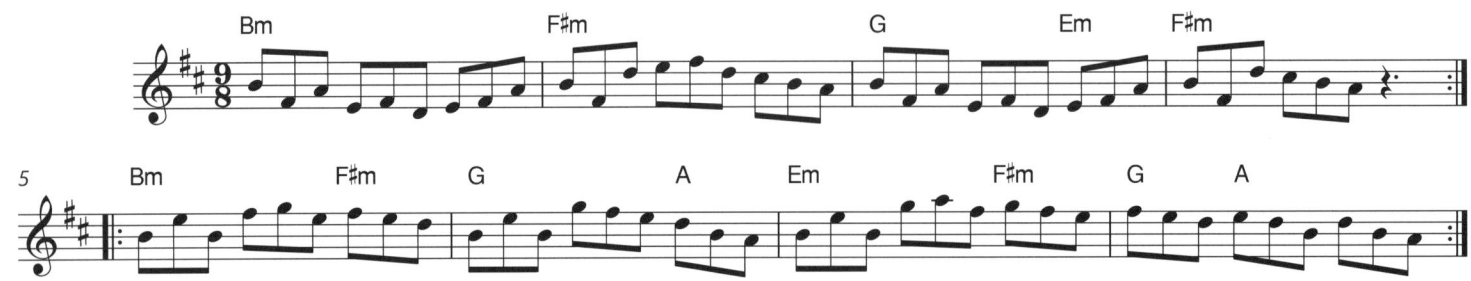

Hornpipes

These tunes really swing! In many areas hornpipes are played with an extremely dotted rhythm, in other places they are played a bit straighter. We have chosen not to exert a blanket editorial policy of writing them one way or the other but have left it up to each composer to notate them as she sees fit. Hornpipes are a firm favourite with me and many other clog dancers, and some great steps have been danced to this type of tune.

Amy Thatcher

THE BEACHCOMBER
Composed by Kerry Russell

Written while remembering the abiding joy of searching, and finding, treasures on many shores.

THE DEVIL'S SCHOTTIS
Composed by Vicki Swan

This tune was written for a telling of the story of the Standing Stones of Stanton Drew. The tune represents the beguiling melody that the devil plays to keep all the guests at a wedding dancing onto the Sabbath and ultimately to their deaths. If you look carefully, you can find the devil's interval in the B part...
TT: Vicki plays this tune for hopstep dances and really gives it that hopstep hornpipe feel.

100 DAYS
Composed by Anna Massie

I spent lockdown 2020 at home with my parents in Fortrose, on the Black Isle, where I kept a daily vlog – The Black Isle Correspondent. This hornpipe was written to mark our 100th episode, when we had a tea party in the garden, tied balloons to the collars of our trusty Labradors and played tunes.

JOLLY ROGER
Composed by Pam Bishop

This tune was written for my band to have a new hornpipe in their repertoire.

MYNYDD DU
Composed by Lucy Rivers

Translates as Black Mountain. Inspired by the black mountains where I grew up
and also heavily inspired by my love of Cajun music – lots of double stopping.

NEUKETYNEUKS
Composed by Fiona Driver

This hornpipe is named after a famous old lane in Kirkwall, Orkney. The tune became well travelled when
Troy MacGillivray and Shane Cook put it on an award-winning album and played it around the world.

TWEEDMOUTH HORNPIPE
Composed by Susie Cochrane

The 'Tweedmouth Hornpipe' was written for my friend Cheryl Stewart's birthday. She is an inspirational dance teacher, choreographer and Northumbrian clogger, who lives in Tweedmouth.

UNCLE ALAN'S CURTSY
Composed by Marina Dodgson

For a much-loved uncle who made up magical tales of his former life. He convinced us that he was so important that my sister and I ought to curtsy as we passed his house on the way to school!

VIEW FROM THE DAM

Composed by Adèle Commins

This hornpipe was composed after a visit to the manmade Spelga Dam in Co. Down following a glorious trip through the Mourne Mountains on a summer day, and I wondered in awe at the expanse of the construction and the lost homes beneath the water.

Reels

I love a reel! They're typically written in 4/4 time but counted in 2/2 as the crotchets are FAST! They're tunes for dancing, and so much more. In Scottish music alone, there are various ways of approaching reels: swingy pipes reels which feel almost dotted; elegant North-East tunes; fast and furious Shetland reels! There's a lovely mix of styles in this selection, and while many of them work as pedal-to-the-metal fast tunes, it's worth exploring swing and tempo while making your way through them – you might find the perfect tune for ceilidh dancing, or the ideal slow reel for a laid-back session.

Anna Massie

AGAINST TIME

Composed by Éadaoin Ní Mhaicín

I wrote this tune on the harp during lockdown 2021.
I later recorded it as part of my debut harp single, 'Against Time'.

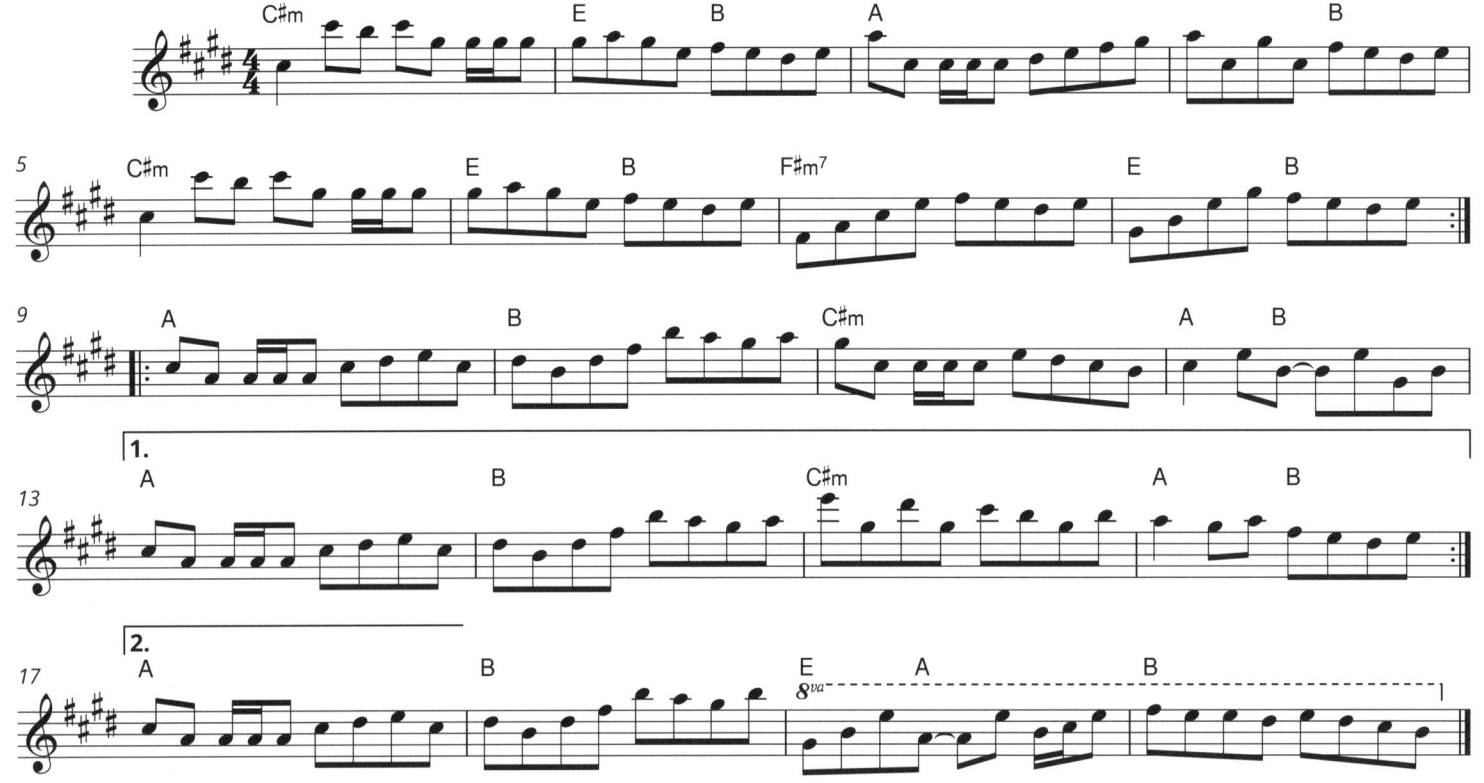

ANGUS GRANT SINGS THE GRATEFUL DEAD

Composed by Sarah McFadyen

I wrote this tune around 2002 while couch surfing at fiddlers Eilidh Shaw & Angus Grant's flat on Easter Road, Edinburgh.
Many a day Angus and mandolinist Luke Plumb would be singing songs of The Grateful Dead in the kitchen.

BACK HOME IN ÖNSBACKEN

Composed by Karen Tweed

While touring in Sweden, I spent a lot of time with Eva Kvarnström and Svante Nordlander –
often ending up in their cosy kitchen for tunes, talks and enormous fun.
This tune celebrates that time, that house and their love.

DA FIDDLER FAE SOOTHOWER

Composed by Margaret Robertson

Written for a great friend, Kerry Russell, on the occasion of her 50th birthday.
It was written after Kerry moved from Shetland to the Scottish Mainland, hence 'soothower' (south)!
This tune is in a Shetland traditional style.

CISSY MIDDLETON OF GAWTHROP

Composed by Carolyn Francis

Cissy Middleton lived in Gawthrop, Dentdale and died in her nineties. She spent her life in the dale farming, gardening, playing the organ in church and exemplifying rural culture. On the way to her funeral on February 14, 2009, this melody appeared in my mind and I named it for her.

TT: This arrangement is part of the repertoire of the Lakeland Fiddlers, a community music group set up by Carolyn in 1998 and still going strong. The two parts are mainly in octaves and it sounds great with loads of fiddle players really going for it!

DUSSELDRAM
Composed by Cathy Geldard

This tune was written after a trip to Dusseldorf with some pipers to play at Musikfest Des Bundeswehr. After a very long rehearsal playing in flat keys we had a lovely evening watching the sunset drinking wine by the Rhein.

FÀILTE
Composed by Anna-Wendy Stevenson

Fàilte, meaning 'welcome', is a reel from 'Suite Uist' which I recorded in 2017 with the Far Flung Collective.

THE FIRST RULE OF BOX CLUB

Composed by Mairearad Green

Written when I was playing in the Scottish accordion band, Box Club –
The First Rule of Box Club is to tell everybody about Box Club!

FOUR FOR A BOY

Composed by Alison Jones

I finished this reel out on a walk, thinking about my son coming home for a holiday.
Then four magpies landed on the path right in front of me. The name of the tune seemed obvious…

GEN-Z

Composed by Imogen Bose-Ward

I have synaesthesia and often see tunes in colour, and this tune seemed be a mustardy yellow colour, which is apparently known as the colour for Generation Z according to an article I read once (so it must definitely be true?!). I like tunes to have a laid back and relaxed feel, and this tune feels nice and lazy.

GRANNY IN THE ATTIC

Composed by Sarah Allen

This reel is dedicated to my Granny in Australia, though she didn't live in an attic.
*TT: This tune tends to be played slower than most reels, and with a real swing to the rhythm.
It's on the Flook album* Rubai, *if you want to hear how it's done!*

GREY DAYS
Composed by Chloë Bryce

This is a tune I wrote for guitarist, Luc McNally, after discovering a shared appreciation for the grey weather in Glasgow. There is something comforting (even joyous?!) about the stillness that comes with a grey day.

JOHNNIE ARMSTRONG (OOR WEE SURPRISE)
Composed by Patsy Seddon

This tune is for the son of my friends Tam and Mary. Johnnie was unexpected and has been delighting them ever since. The tune is meant to be in the style of the music of the Scottish Borders where the Armstrongs are from.

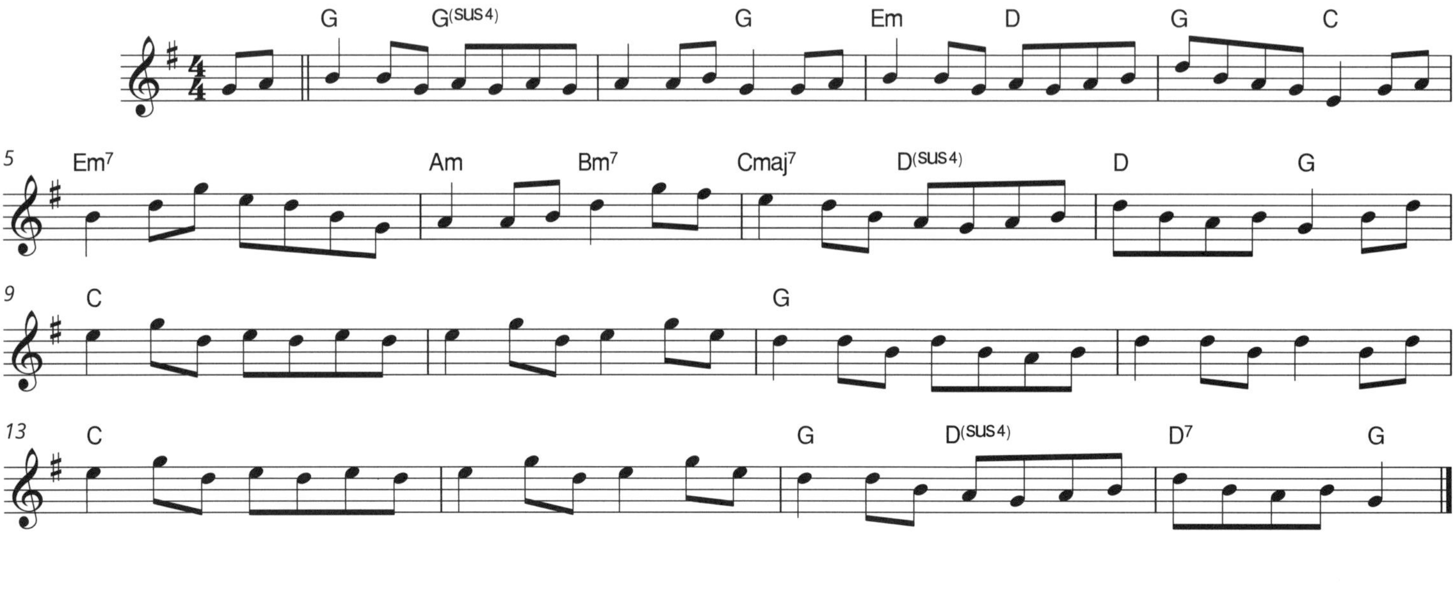

HOLTWOOD REEL
Composed by Jess Arrowsmith

This reel was written in 1997 while in the shared house I lived in at the time, on Holtwood Road in Sheffield.

LADY ISABELLA
Composed by Lauren MacColl

Written as part of 'The Seer' – music inspired by the life and prophecies of the Brahan Seer.
Lady Isabella, wife of the 3rd Earl of Seaforth, supposedly ordered the death of the 17th century prophet.
Her portrait hangs in Fortrose Town Hall.

LAID BACK LIZ

Composed by Eilidh Steel

Composed for Irish-American fiddle player, Liz Carroll.

LINDA'S LILT

Composed by Margaret Robertson

Written for an Australian friend and fiddler, Linda Rankin, for her 50th birthday which was celebrated in Scotland.

NEVER TRUST GOOGLE MAPS

Composed by Isla Ratcliff

Never trust Google Maps to get to the Glencoe Square Dance in Cape Breton.
We found ourselves lost on a 9km dirt track road, but at least it provided a lot of laughs!

NEW YEAR'S RESOLUTIONS

Composed by Mairéad Carey

I wrote this tune around the New Year and decided to call it after the long list of resolutions people make every year.
This tune was performed as part of the inaugural Quercus Scholarship Gala night in University College Cork.

PARMOGEDDON
Composed by Grace Smith

I wrote this reel in 2012 for a really fun band I played with at the time.
It's named in honour of a Teesside food speciality, the Parmo.

THE PINNACLE
Composed by Christine Edwards

The Pinnacle is a residential building in the city centre on Bothwell Street, Glasgow.

THE PORT DASH
Composed by Róisín Ward Morrow

We often take our dog on a walk to Port Beach, which is near Clogherhead in Co. Louth. This reel was inspired by watching him run through waves and chase seagulls, free and up to no good!

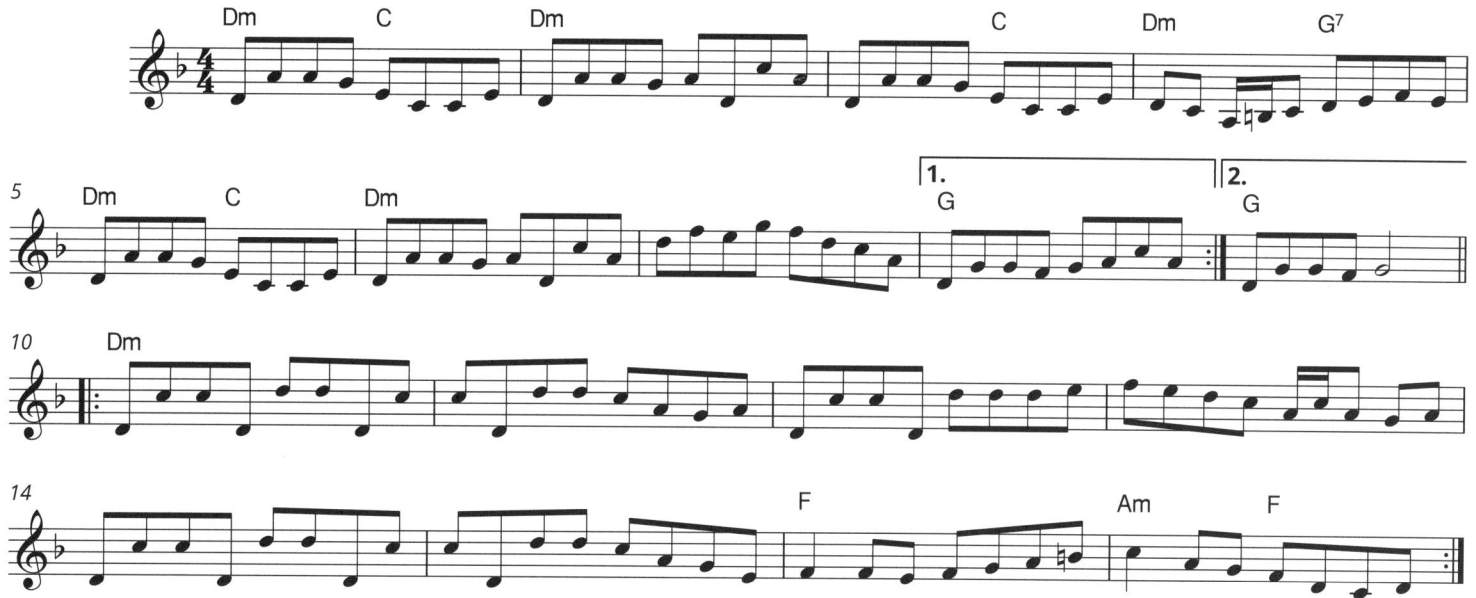

THE RED CROW
Composed by Mairéad Ní Mhaonaigh

'The Red Crow' is a tune based on the Donegal Fiddle tradition where the lower strings are played to give a drone effect like the Low Highland and the Twenty One Highland. It gives a great rasp to the instrument!

THUGAINN
Composed by Patsy Reid

'Thugainn' was part of a commission from Highland Council for their Youth Symphony Orchestra and folk band, Snas to perform. It's a 3-part slow reel. I suppose the differences between parts are quite subtle but to me there are distinct differences, with a continuous build throughout.

TRIPOD'S FROLICS
Composed by Tina Jordan Rees

This reel is named after a lovely little three-legged kitty who adopted us for a while.

THE UNDERWATER GARDENER
Composed by Sarah Northcott

A reel for my good friend and rainy-day gardening pal Bryan Astor, written in a tent on a clifftop in Donegal.
A perfect example of tune evolution – Sarah-Jane Summers recorded a beautiful slow version on her album *Nesta*.

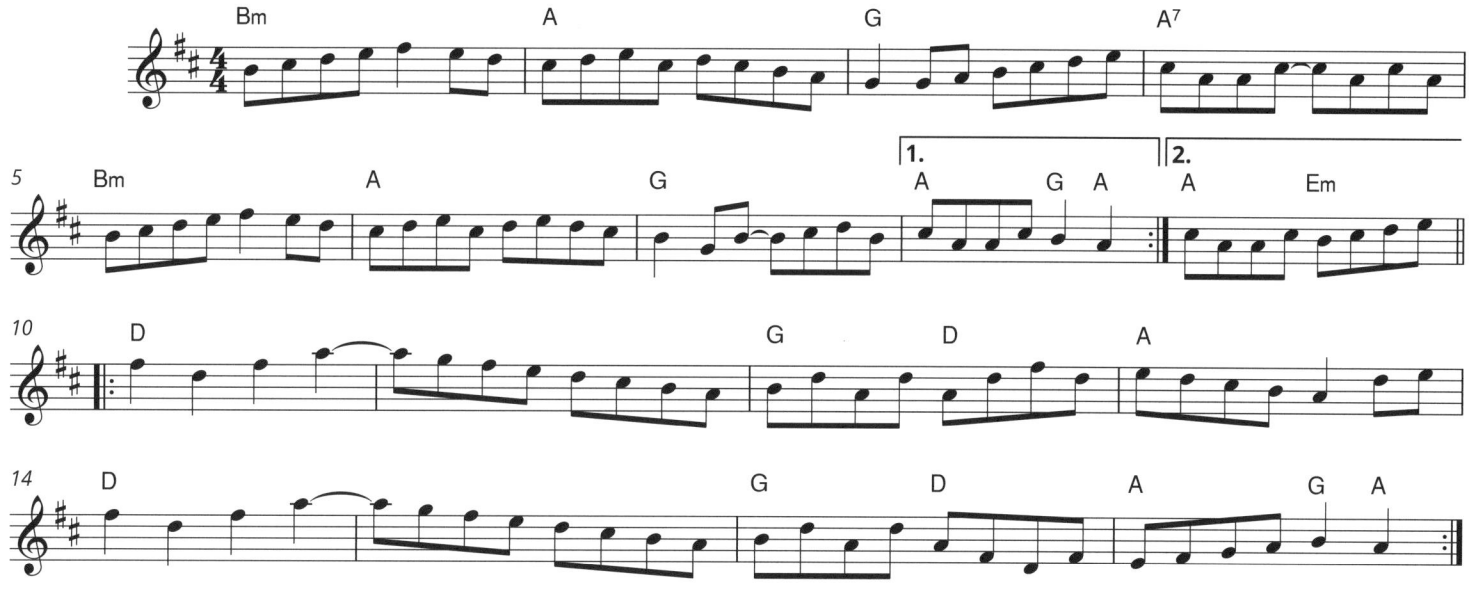

THE WELCOME HOME
Composed by Kathryn Tickell

Self-explanatory for anyone who goes away from home a lot. It's always good to come back.
TT: Kathryn wrote this on the Northumbrian pipes, a transposing instrument which sound a tone lower than the written music, so don't be alarmed if you try playing along with her CD and it sounds very strange!

Y SELAR

Composed by Angharad Jenkins

A lively little tune in homage to the Welsh language pop/rock magazine I used to read regularly as a teenager. Wales's Welsh language pop scene is thriving and youthful and has had a huge part to play in maintaining Welsh as a contemporary, living language.

Marches

As the name suggests, marches were originally written for marching to, and tend to have a very strong and regular rhythm. They can be written in any time signature but in folk and traditional music are most commonly in 4/4, 3/4, 2/4 and 6/8.

There is a surprisingly wide tempo range: many Scottish pipe marches have a military background, so the tempo matches the pace of the soldiers walking in step. Other influences might include regional styles, dance requirements and/or the personal preferences of the musicians. For example, Lauren MacColl says, as a performance piece, she prefers a slightly slower tempo for her march, 'Tune for Jean', and when I play 2/4 marches for ceilidh dances at home in Achiltibuie we play all the tunes for 'The Canadian Barn Dance' much faster than for the same dance elsewhere!

Although the more contemporary marches are often not written expressly for the same practical dancing or marching purposes, the ingrained rhythms are there, and you will certainly enjoy the movement of all of these fantastic marches.

Mairearad Green

A FAR AWAY REBEL
Composed by Adèle Commins

This march was written while thinking about a good friend who was on a trip to the 'Rebel County' of Co. Cork. My writing of marches has always been inspired by Brian O'Kane as we played many of his marches in our céilí bands for fleadhanna.

A TUNE FOR JEAN
Composed by Lauren MacColl

During the first lockdown, I was involved in a virtual festival for Fèis Rois. This slow march was written for an online auction to raise funds for the arts organisation. It was named 'A Tune for Jean' by the winning bidder.

ALAN FRIENDLY
Composed by Corrina Hewat

Written for Alan Caldwell, an extraordinary man with an extraordinary wife
and three girls who all make the world a better place.

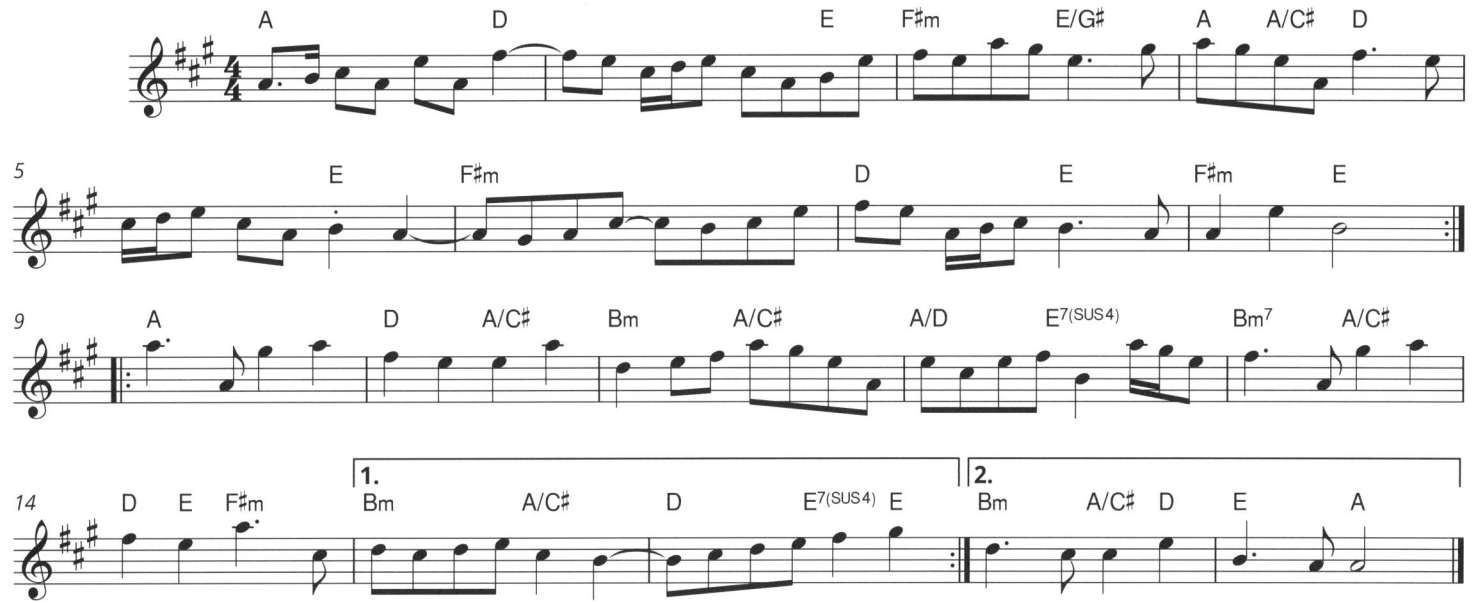

ARTHUR'S SEAT
Composed by Anna-Wendy Stevenson

A march composed as part of my 2005 New Voices commission 'My Edinburgh',
inspired by the beautiful city I grew up in, and where I have enjoyed playing in many sessions!

BECCY'S BIG DAY
Composed by Olivia Ross

This 3/4 march was written for a very good friend, Rebecca Amphlett, (now Amer) who got married on 7th August 2021. It was a wonderful day!

THE GREAT EXODUS
Composed by Gráinne Brady

This tune is featured on my first album *The Road Across the Hills*.

THE HALSWAY PARADE
Composed by Vicki Swan

I have run nyckelharpa courses at Halsway Manor since 2012 and it has become tradition that towards the end of the course we parade en masse down to a mosaic in the gardens. This is the tune that all the participants get taught and is catchy and easy enough for everyone to be able to play.

JOHN MacDOUGALL'S MARCH
Composed by Amy Geddes

This march for John MacDougall was written in 2017. John and his wife Sheena attended a charity event I was playing at and as part of the fundraising auction I donated a tune commission. John won the bid and asked for a waltz for Sheena, but he is a piper, and they were more than generous, so I decided to write a tune suitable for pipes as well as a waltz.

PIPE MAJOR BOBBY COGHILL OF WICK

Composed by Eilidh Steel

This is a 2/4 pipe march that I wrote for the late Bobby Coghill while he was a tutor of mine at college.
He was a lovely and talented man who played pipes, accordion and fiddle,
well known in the pipe band and Scottish dance band scenes.

PAPERWORK SUCKS
Composed by Sophy Ball

Throwing my hands up in frustration after heaps of e-mails and organising, I played this angrily on my fiddle and felt much better. I highly recommend it as a break from any annoying and frustrating activity.

SHEILA & GORDON'S GOLDEN WEDDING MARCH
Composed by Marie Fielding

This march is an example of my love for Cape Breton style tunes.
This was a commission for a Golden Wedding Anniversary which felt very special to be part of.

SOCIETY'S WELCOME TO THE YEAR '21

Composed by Claire Gullan

A 12/8 pipe style march written in A Dorian mode to fit with the pipes. I think the character of this tune conveys both the hope and horror that society entered into the year 2021 with – a year of uncertainty, mid pandemic.

Polkas

Fast, lively tunes, often surprisingly simple but really effective when you want to notch things up a bit! Polkas are usually in 2/4, English polkas tend to be in 4/4 and a bit slower, and two of our composers submitted tunes in 3/4 which they think of as polkas, and who am I to disagree? I like the idea that perhaps 'polka', as well as being a type of dance, could also be an intention, a state of mind, a kind of upbeat intensity?!

Kathryn Tickell

THE BALLYMENA POLKA
Composed by Ailie Robertson
This tune was written after a trip to Ballymena in Co. Antrim.

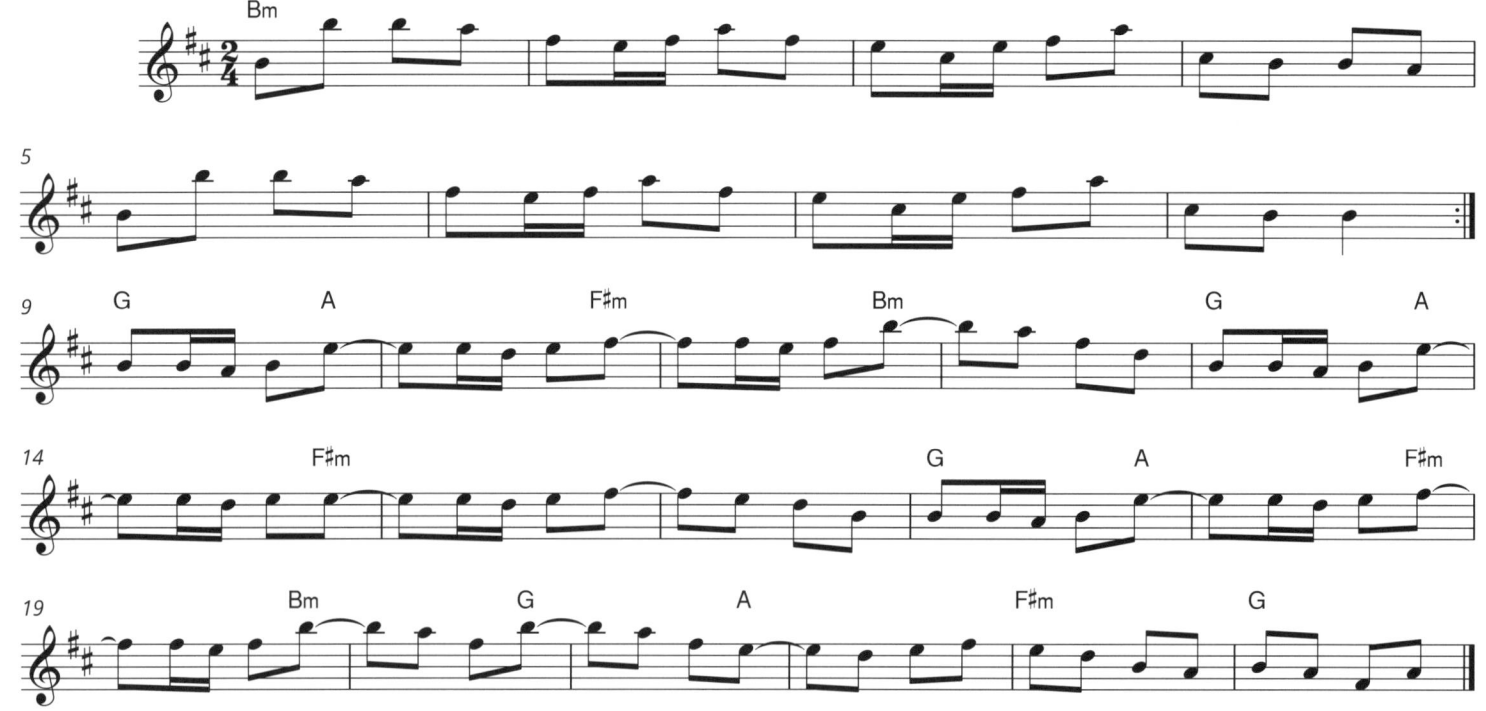

BYDDWCH YN GAREDIG
Composed by Mari Morgan

'Byddwch yn Garedig' (Be Kind) was inspired by seeing children being nice and not so nice to each other,
which is mirrored in the switch between the G mixolydian and G minor keys.
It can be played with company if you like and stamping your feet.

CROW ROAD CROFT
Composed by Lauren MacColl

I lived on Glasgow's Crow Road for five years after music college and did my best to turn
a modern flat into a wee Highland home with tweeds and woolly blankets.
I've recorded this with both RANT and the flautist Calum Stewart.
*TT: We're more used to seeing polkas in 2/4 but Lauren insists she's "always thought of this one as a 3/4 polka
– definitely more upbeat than a waltz" so into the Polka section it goes…*

THE LOCKDOWN POLKA
Composed by Maeve McCann

This tune came out of me during the dark winter lockdown of 2021. I had been messing around thinking
I might write a jig or a reel, but a polka came out instead. I realised then that I was very deprived of a dance!

PUCK GOES DANCING

Composed by Harriet Power

This tune is a fast polka inspired by Les Zeoles' quirky polka, 'L'atelier'.

SEASON'S PROMISE

Composed by Laurel Swift

I wrote this tune as a tool for teaching variation but play it loads as it's such a joyful little piece!
There are tips on where to start with variations on my YouTube channel.
TT: We've put this in the polkas section because it works so well as an English polka, but Laurel also plays it as a reel. When playing for dancing she often substitutes polkas for reels and says that this tune fits well for ceilidh classics such as 'The Norfolk Square Dance', 'Duck The Oyster' or 'Circassian Circle'.

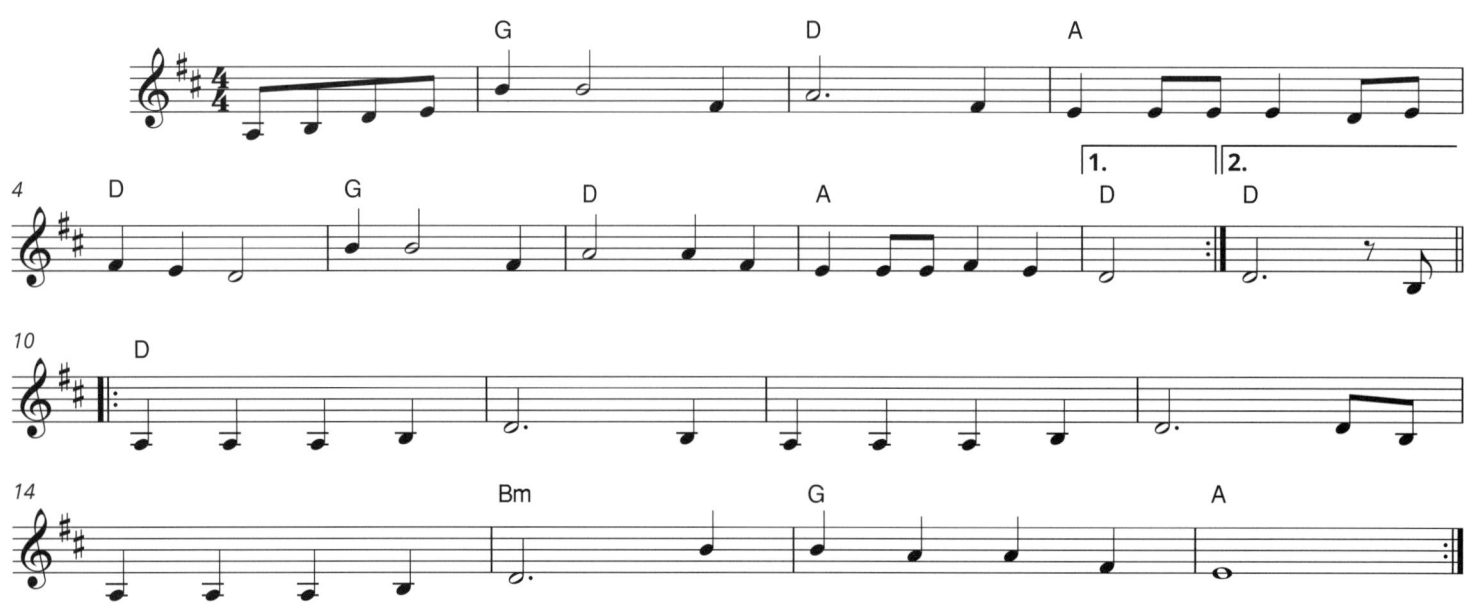

THE SHORES OF LOCH AWE
Composed by Karen Woods

The first glimmers of this polka came to me whilst playing fiddle in the kitchen the morning before travelling to Scotland for a holiday on the shores of Loch Awe. It was in early March 2020, just before the pandemic and first lockdown. We had a spectacular journey through the snow-covered mountains and stunning landscape of greens and browns of the west of Scotland. During our stay in a beautiful wooden loch side cabin, I completed the tune.

THE TWO-PART POUR POLKA
Composed by Niamh Ní Charra

I composed this polka especially for our Bodhrán player Dom Keogh who loves his Guinness. We performed one year at a Guinness-sponsored festival outside of Ireland. As we played, we could see the bar at the back where audience members were ordering pints. Dom was horrified and quite distracted at the manner in which the bartenders were pulling the pints so I temporarily renamed one of my other compositions the 'Two-Part Pour' so that I could diplomatically instruct them from the stage, much to Dom's amusement and relief. We both decided this diplomatic intervention might be required again in the future, hence this new polka. The festival, of course, shall remain nameless!

UP THE LUM

Composed by Rachel Newton

This tune and 'Eggshell Brewery' (p104) were written as part of my New Voices Commission for
Celtic Connections, *Changeling*, which is also the name of my third album. Lum is the Scots word for chimney.
*TT: On the harp Rachel just plays an A pedal throughout the A part
and then a rising bass D, E, F natural, G (one per bar) for the B part.*

WILBUR'S WONDER

Composed by Sue Harris

My youngest grandson was born in February 2020, and I got to see him just once before we were
all locked down. So, I set to and wrote this tune for him. He is a wonder of course,
and we have a polka around together when they come to visit me.

Waltzes & Mazurkas

We have put these two tune types together as they are often interchangeable. The main difference relates to playing for dancing, where the tempo of the tune tells the dancing audience whether to dance a waltz or a mazurka.

Across mainland Europe waltzes are often danced quite fast and their character is a smooth swirl. Mazurkas tend to be slower with a rise and fall motion that is created by the unique mazurka step. In the UK, speeds vary depending on whether tunes are being used in a ceilidh, barn dance, ball dance or concert, and as usual with folk music this can change from region to region.

There can also be a crossover between waltzes and slow airs; the same tune can be played in two very different ways. If you are not playing for dancing, you don't have to worry about any of that. You can just explore these beautiful tunes and let them tell you what speed they want to be played at!

Jo Freya

A GIRL ON THE ROCK
Composed by Kate Strudwick

Playing at Jo Harding's 80th birthday party I saw a photo of her as a child standing on a rock.
Her stance and direct gaze marked her out as someone who was going to be amazing – and she is.

A TUNE FOR LEWIS
Composed by Kirstie McLanaghan

Written for my precious son Lewis who died by suicide on the 15th May 2021.
A few days after Lew died, I picked up my fiddle, started to play and this tune came out.
I played it to him on the evening before his funeral and he took a copy with him.

ANOTHER DAY
Composed by Karen Gledhill

This is second in a series of three lockdown pieces – the most optimistic of the three.
A moment of wistful reflection amongst the relentless days of the winter of 2020.

THE CALM BETWEEN THE STORMS
Composed by Martha Woods

This tune can be played as a waltz or a slow air. Its changing thirds give a feeling of uncertainty.

BERT MACKENZIE'S 70TH BIRTHDAY WALTZ
Composed by Louise Mackenzie

Written for my dad's 70th birthday. As a youngster, he started farming life as a ploughman and worked with Clydesdale horses to plough the fields. He sang traditional songs and whistled as a source of entertainment, and his love of music continued throughout his life.

CASTLE HILL
Composed by Delyth Jenkins

Castle Hill is part of the Long Mynd range that straddles the border between Wales and England. I wrote this tune in memory of my parents, who enjoyed walking there together and that is where their ashes are scattered.

BRESYCHEN DDIOG
Composed by Elsa Davies
'Bresychen Ddiog' is a Mazurka.

ELVASTON CASTLE
Composed by Jess Arrowsmith
This tune was written as a wedding present for good friends Paul and Vicky Baker when they were married at, you guessed it, Elvaston Castle in Derbyshire in 2000.

THE CHRISTMAS EVE WALTZ

Composed by Marie Fielding

This tune was composed for an album *An Seisiún*, recorded in Dingle Ireland with Donogh Hennessy and Tom Orr around 2012. It's a relaxed waltz that I'd like to think suits most instruments and simple enough to enjoy.

KEY WORKERS WALTZ
Composed by Angharad Jenkins

In March 2020 Andrew de Salis commissioned me to write this tune for his sister, Ailsa Johnstone of Pathhead, Midlothian, who is a nurse in the Borders General Hospital near Edinburgh. It's also of course dedicated to all the wonderful key workers who worked tirelessly throughout the pandemic.

LEAVING WHITBY
Composed by Helen Bell

Written in the back of a car, heading home from Whitby Folk Festival in the early 2000s.
TT: This waltz also sounds beautiful slowed down and played as an air.

74

LURAND
Composed by Heather Woodbridge

Lurand is the name of my family home, a renovated crofthouse in North Ronaldsay.
In 2012 I had the privilege to study Musikk in Voss, Norway and I wrote
this tune for the home I was about to leave for the first time.

MAGGIE WEST'S WALTZ
Composed by Mairearad Green

A tune for my grandmother, Margaret Macleod from West of the township of Achnahaird, Wester Ross.

MAZURKA
Composed by Catrin Ashton

I wrote this tune a long time ago. I can't remember a thing about its conception,
but I maintain that a mazurka is one of the finest dances ever invented.

MIKE & CATHERINE'S
Composed by Isla Callister

I wrote this tune during a 2-week isolation stint during the pandemic in 2020. A lovely couple kindly let me
stay in their flat for the duration – so I wrote them this wee waltz as a thank you!

MAZURKA IN THE DARK
Composed by Harriet Power

This tune was inspired by some magical late-night dancing I stumbled across at the French festival Le Son Continu. The dancers were on a small stage in the middle of the woods, lit by a single candle.

PANDEMONIUM
Composed by Rebecca McCarthy-Kent

This tune was composed as part of 'Tradchestra', a summer orchestra set up by the McCarthy-Kent Family in Tramore, Co. Waterford. I wrote it in June 2021 to reflect the struggles and upset caused by the Covid-19 pandemic. It was the first time many of these young musicians were being brought back together to play after 18 months, so this tune represents this drought of music from their lives.

OTIS & DEANIE
Composed by Sarah McFadyen

Written for dear friends from Cape Breton. Otis Tomas is a master luthier and tunesmith, and Deanie Cox is a beautiful potter. In 2009 I was fortuitous enough to make my own fiddle with Otis as my guide.

ROSA'S WALTZ
Composed by Delyth Jenkins

I wrote this tune as a welcome-to-the-world present for my great niece Rosa Delyth. My dad said: 'Had to get a Welsh name in there and where better to look for inspiration!' And what better reason to write a tune!

STEVE FISHER'S LAMENT

Composed by Mel Biggs

I found this tune in an old squeezebox that I inherited through The Morris. Steve Fisher was a musician for North Wales Morris sides. I never knew Steve but felt a connection to him through my custodianship of his instrument. I had it restored and was rewarded with this melody.

SWIRLING FLAMES
Composed by Jo Freya

This is a mazurka. I wrote it specifically for a summer school I was tutoring on at Halsway Manor where the theme for the week was fire. One of the tutors, Paul Hutchinson, liked it so much that he started teaching it in his accordion groups in the UK and his zoom accordion group in Australia.

TOO CUTE TO CORRECT
Composed by Amy Thatcher

Named after the way my two-year-old twins pronounce things incorrectly (or choose another word altogether) and not only is it too cute to correct, but the whole family ends up switching to their version!

THE TRIP TO GORTHLECK

Composed by Mary Macmaster

This tune was written for Katie and Steve, my sister and her husband.

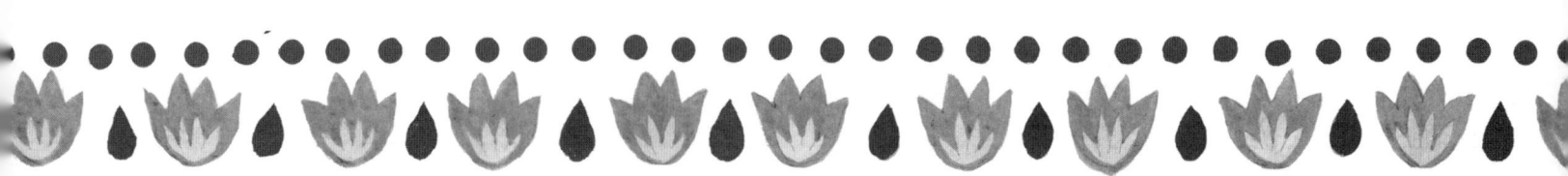

WALTZING AT GIGGLESWICK

Composed by Rachael McShane

This was commissioned for the 10th anniversary of the charity Music 4 People that I'm a proud patron of. They run a lovely summer school in Yorkshire in a place called Giggleswick, one of the many great Yorkshire place names! Recorded on *When All Is Still* by Rachael McShane & The Cartographers.

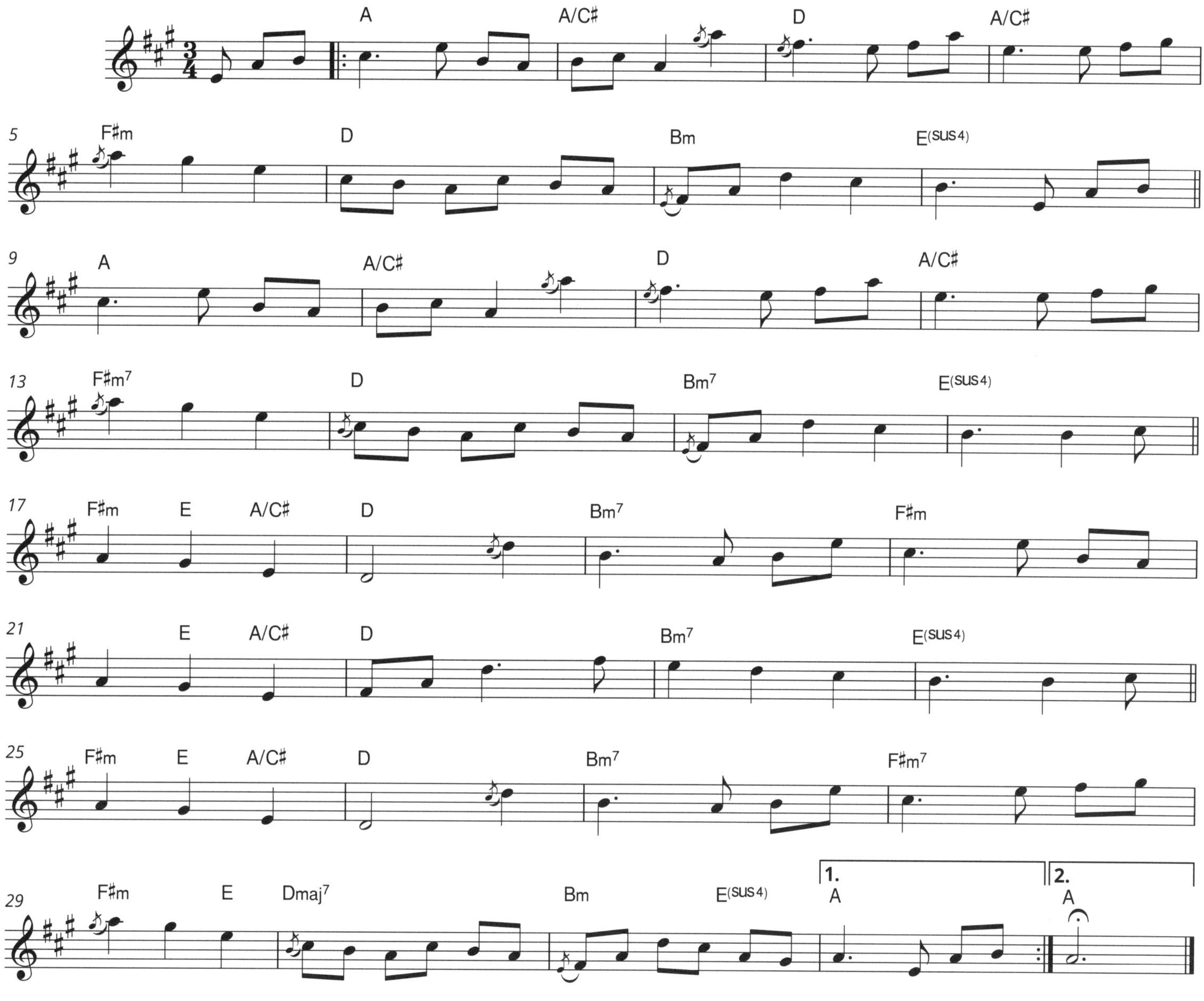

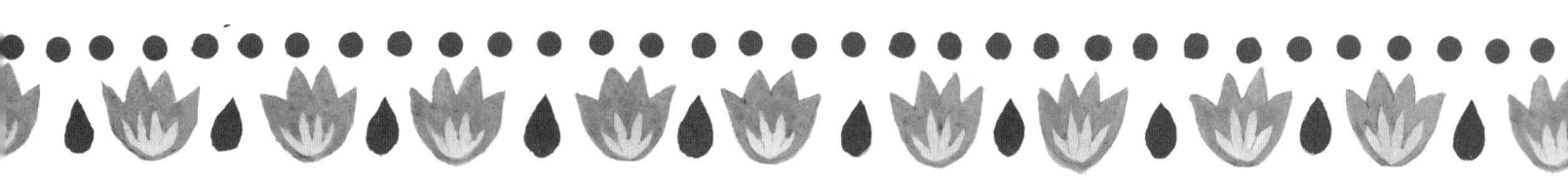

Crooked Tunes

Sometimes if you are writing a tune in your head or on your instrument, it's not until you start to write it down that you realise your tune has decided to give itself a little bar or two of different lengths to all the others. This can happen quite naturally – the melody sometimes just wants to have a little longer (or less) on a certain phrase. Or perhaps you set out to write a tune with a little 'skip' in it, or something that will disrupt the usual rhythmic pattern, like Zoë Conway's coda to 'Rounding Malin Head' which gives the player and accompanist a bit of added rhythmic interest for a bit of a flourish at the end!

Kathryn Tickell

BONFIRE NIGHT
Composed by Helen Gentile

The irregular rhythms in this tune are inspired by the unpredictable flickering of flames, whilst the bright major key brings to mind the convivial ambience of sharing heat, light and merriment around the bonfire.
TT: Helen originally wrote this for bombarde in B♭, but she doesn't mind if you want to transpose it to D or something more suitable for your instrument.

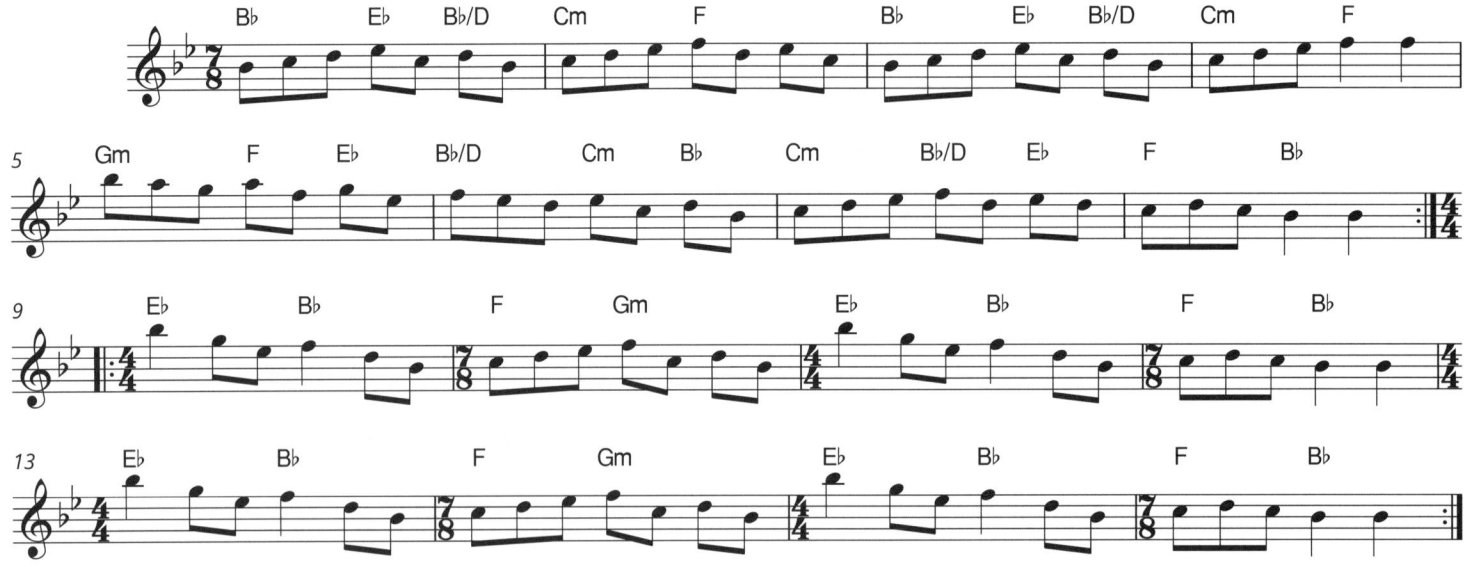

LOCH NAN CLIADHEAMHAN
Composed by Rachel Newton

I wrote this tune as part of a wider commission about the area of Coigach and Assynt. It's inspired by the Tobar an Dualchais recording of Alexander Maclean telling the story of Loch nan Claidheamhan (Loch of the Swords). The men of Assynt and Coigach fought over ownership of Inverpolly.
After the battle the men of Coigach having won threw their swords in the Loch.
TT: Rachel plays this tune as a kind of slow jig.

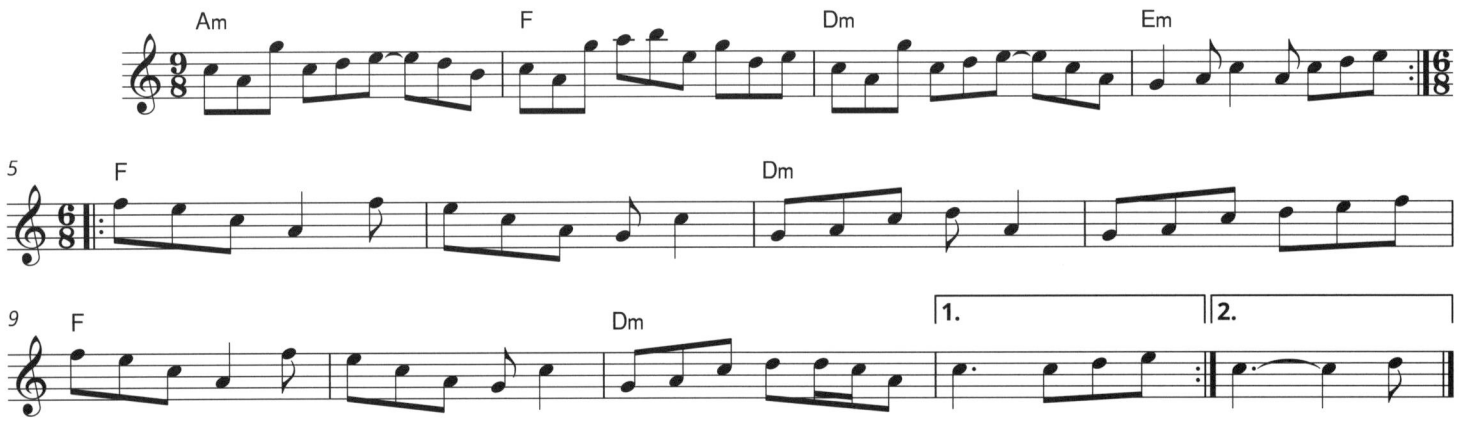

HAUL AR Y CARREG
(SUN ON THE STONE)
Composed by Stacey Blythe

I wrote this on a ukulele in Spain. A small lizard sat on a rock in the sunshine listening to me
(I thought!) as I found the melody. As soon as I stopped it skipped away into the shade.

MR COLLINS' NO. 2
Composed by Jess Arrowsmith

'Mr Collins' No. 2' was written for Pecsaetan to dance to. It follows the unusual format (with a 10 bar B music)
of traditional tune Black Joak, from the Cotswold Morris tradition of Ilmington. Its first public outing (along with its
sister tune 'Mr Collins' No. 1') was at a memorial concert for singer Johnny Collins in 2010, hence the name(s).

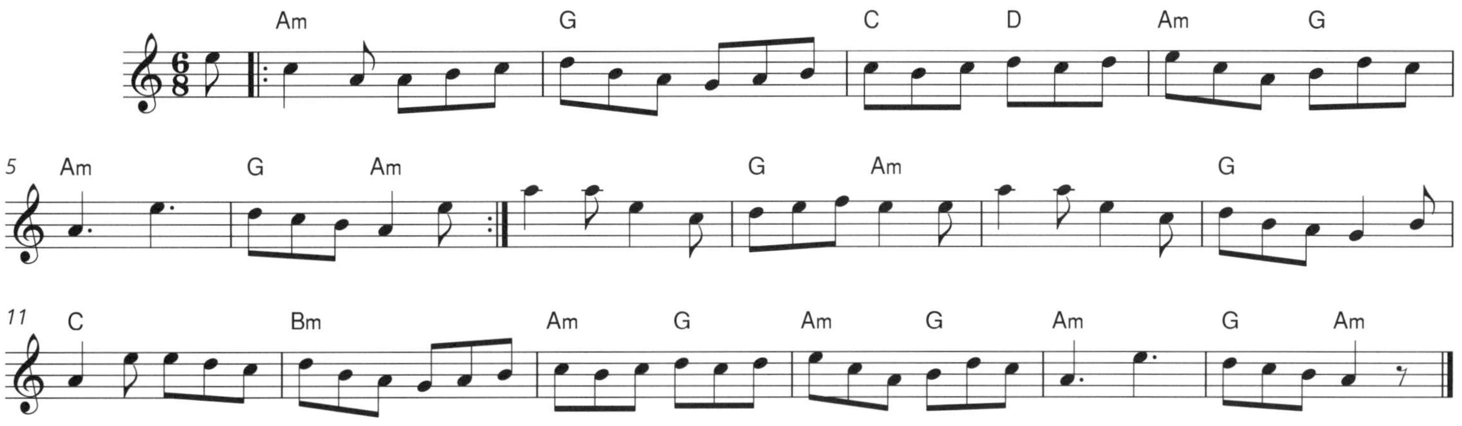

THE JOY OF IT!
Composed by Catriona Macdonald

A tune celebrating the feeling you get when music carries you away to a happy place.
*TT: Fiddle players – these bowings will help you get the right swing and groove for this tune.
Catriona plays it faster than a waltz, and with the fiddle tuned AEAE which gives a great ring to the sound.*

LA FEMME DU SAULE
Composed by Sarah Northcott

La Femme du Saule (The Willow Woman) is my ancestor Ann Hamlin, a herbalist in Stoke St Gregory, Somerset, in the early eighteenth century. She often used willow bark, which we now know contains aspirin. It sounds a bit French...

OLD WAX JACKET
Composed by Tamsin Elliott

'Old Wax Jacket' is a nostalgic smell that reminds me of my childhood friend Will. The B part feels like it has five-beat phrases, but it turns out that you can write it down as alternating bars of 9/8 and 6/8. So there you go. I wrote this on piano accordion, and I tend to vary my bass patterns quite a lot when I'm playing it, particularly in the B part.
TT: Tamsin suggests that you 'be generous with your ornamentation!'

PILLOWFISH
Composed by Helen Bell

The name of this tune came from a misheard reply to the question, "What time is it?" (The actual answer was "ten to eleven" but there was apparently something odd going on with the acoustics of the room.)

THE PHRAYES
Composed by Corrina Hewat

A tune written after meeting and supporting fiddler Martin Hayes and guitarist Denis Cahill on a gig at the Highland Music Festival in Dingwall. It was trying to express the elusive and transporting Martin Hayes phrasing of melodies. This tune literally wrote itself, as if a string of notes from the air passed through and spilled onto the harp and I had to quickly give them space to be.

THE REST AND BE THANKFUL

Composed by Marit Fält

This is a piece written for my New Voices commission 'Irrationalities'. I composed it shortly after completing chemotherapy, it's a piece of music reflecting my Hodgkins lymphoma journey in 2019. It is also the most beautiful – but slightly scary – road in Argyll.

ROUNDING MALIN HEAD

Composed by Zoë Conway

I was a young teenager when I wrote this reel (in my parents back sitting room) inspired by contemporary Irish traditional music, especially using unusual time signatures and beats skipped or added on. One of the highlights of my musical life was recording this with Bill Whelan on keyboards and Donal Lunny on bouzouki – a magical moment.

THA I AIR SRÀID

Composed by Rona Wilkie

Written during the first Mamiaith minority language residency. A modern and feminist puirt-a-beul, inspired by a photograph of a woman protesting with her son during the Hong Kong riots. The rhythm of the words dictated the melodic composition.

Strange Times

*Traditionally, dance tunes from the islands comprising the UK and Ireland have tended to be in either 2, 3 or 4 per bar. The tunes in this section are moving away from that. Modern performance contexts for folk and traditional music are expanding beyond playing for dancing to complex arrangements destined for the concert stage. As we composers, musicians and dancers have become more familiar with music from further afield, we've become more rhythmically and harmonically adventurous, embracing different time signatures like 5/4 and 7/8. You can think of these as having a slightly lopsided pulse. Often the rhythms are subdivided, so a 5/4 tune might be divided with the emphasis on **1** 2 3, **1** 2 or **1** 2, **1** 2 3. In the score, this can usually be identified by how the stems of the notes have been grouped.*

If you are an accompanist or play an instrument like piano or accordion where you can accompany yourself, it can be very satisfying to work out a cool arrangement exploring these rhythms.

Expect unusual time signatures and irregular structures which don't perhaps fit the usual traditional dance meters. Having said that, we've put a few cracking 3/2 hornpipes in here too. Try pulling shapes to some of these tunes!

Amy Thatcher & Angharad Jenkins

AYE FLY

Composed by Bryony Griffith

Inspired by a fly on a hotel window while on tour in Italy during a torrential storm.
It would potter about for a while then have a mad buzz before chilling out again.

THE DALE

Composed by Grace Smith

I wrote this tune when I moved to the North West, an area associated with lots of 3/2 hornpipes.
This tune ended up becoming more of a Hanter Dro and it always reminds me of an exciting time of change.

CLOGFAENYDD
Composed by Bethan Rhiannon

This was a tune commission from the beginning of lockdown, and it was a great distraction.
I don't tend to have stories behind my tunes, I just write them because it's fun!
TT: We've added some chords to this tune but it all fits over a D drone so just have fun with the rhythms!

DUCKS AT LUSS
Composed by Tina Jordan Rees

Written after watching the ducks at Luss, Loch Lomond.

EMERGENCY OF THE FEMALE KIND

Composed by Amy Thatcher

This tune is about women standing together: the team spirit instead of the mean spirit.
One woman's success isn't another's demise.
*TT: We put this in the 'Strange Times' section after watching Amy playing this and tapping her foot in a completely different rhythm to the chords she plays on the left hand of the accordion.
She is a Queen of complex rhythms!*

FOR MARIE

Composed by Isla Callister

This tune was written for the wonderful fiddler, composer and educator Marie Fielding. She has been a massive source of encouragement, inspiration and support over the last few years, so I decided to dedicate this tune to her.

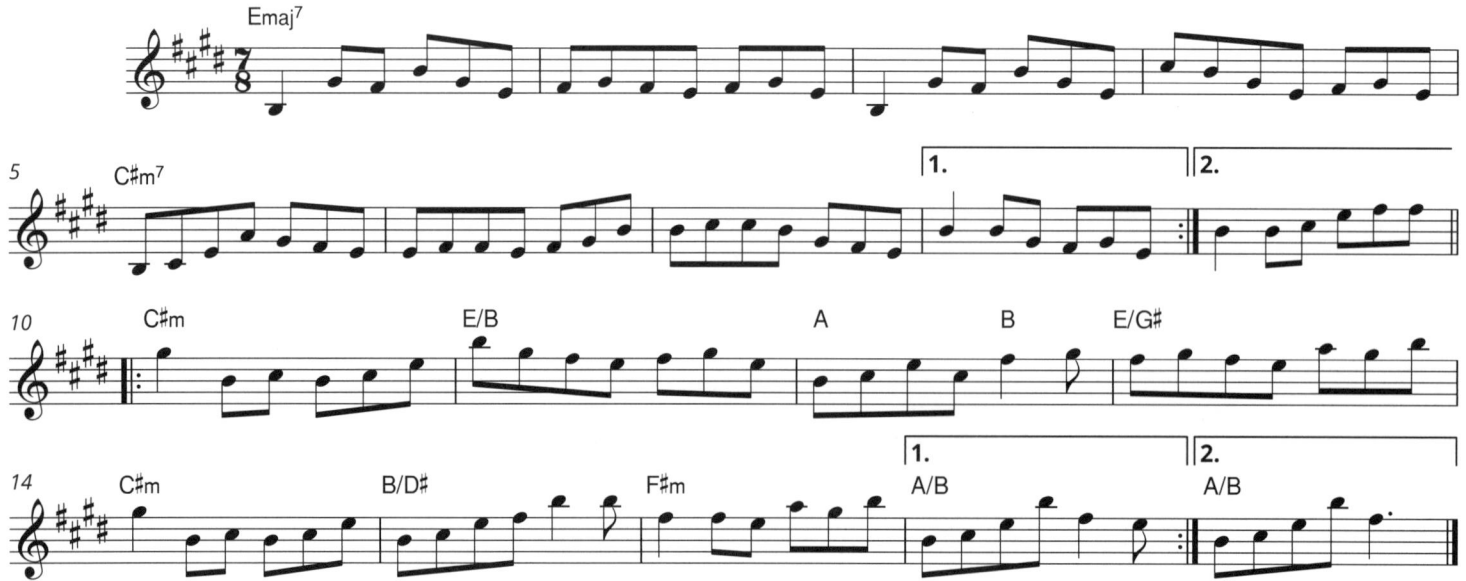

KING BRAMBLE
Composed by Laurel Swift

I love 3/2 hornpipes and am forever trying to write one as cracking as the traditional tune 'Rusty Gulley'!
The B part of 'King Bramble' lends itself to great build and release of tension
and reminds me of one blustery autumn squirrelled away in Wales.

YER PEAKS ARE GETTING PEAKIER
Composed by Laura-Beth Salter

I love playing uneven tunes, particularly those that muck about with the groupings of the notes.
This 5/8 changes groupings every other bar. It's written for my good friend Fiona Dunn
who was in the process of overcoming a tough time. You rock Fi.

LAST TRIP TO DUNBAR

Composed by Catherine Robson

This tune was written after my final visit to my mum's house in Chipping Norton,
Dunbar Cottage, before she moved back to Newcastle.
*TT: Of course you can put your own chords to this tune – or channel your inner
Northumbrian piper and try it with just a D (&A) drone!*

PAW BRAN

Composed by Martha Woods

I wrote 'Paw Bran' (Cornish for 'buttercup') to accompany the kabm pemp (five-step) dance. I am fascinated by how 5/4 tunes have become an important part of Cornwall's musical identity over the last couple of decades!

Here you will find the tunes which don't fit into any other category, maybe because they are unusual in meter, structure or tempo, or perhaps because we didn't have enough of that tune-type to warrant a whole section. You'll find a handful of strathspeys in here, and a couple of beautiful bourrées. There is also Llio Rhydderch's 'Alaw i Nansi' rooted in the Welsh harp 'tune and variations' tradition, which – in essence – are instrumental display pieces: a simple tune set out, with the expectation that it will be developed by the performer, becoming increasingly elaborate with each rendition. But of course, these tunes – as with every tune in the book – can and should be played and enjoyed on any instrument.

Angharad Jenkins

AKAROA

Composed by Annette Davies

A lively, driving tune which I play AB AB AB CD AB CD to build up to the syncopation and chord changes in section D. Geoff Liles and I recorded this on our CD, joined by friends playing hurdy-gurdy and pipes.

ALAW I NANSI (TEYRNGED DISGYBL)
A MELODY FOR NANSI (A PUPIL'S TRIBUTE)
Composed by Llio Rhydderch

I composed this Air and Variations for my teacher and relative, the famous Nansi Richards. It is on my CD *Melangell*, named for the saint whose shrine is in the church at Pennant Melangell. Nansi lies buried in the churchyard.

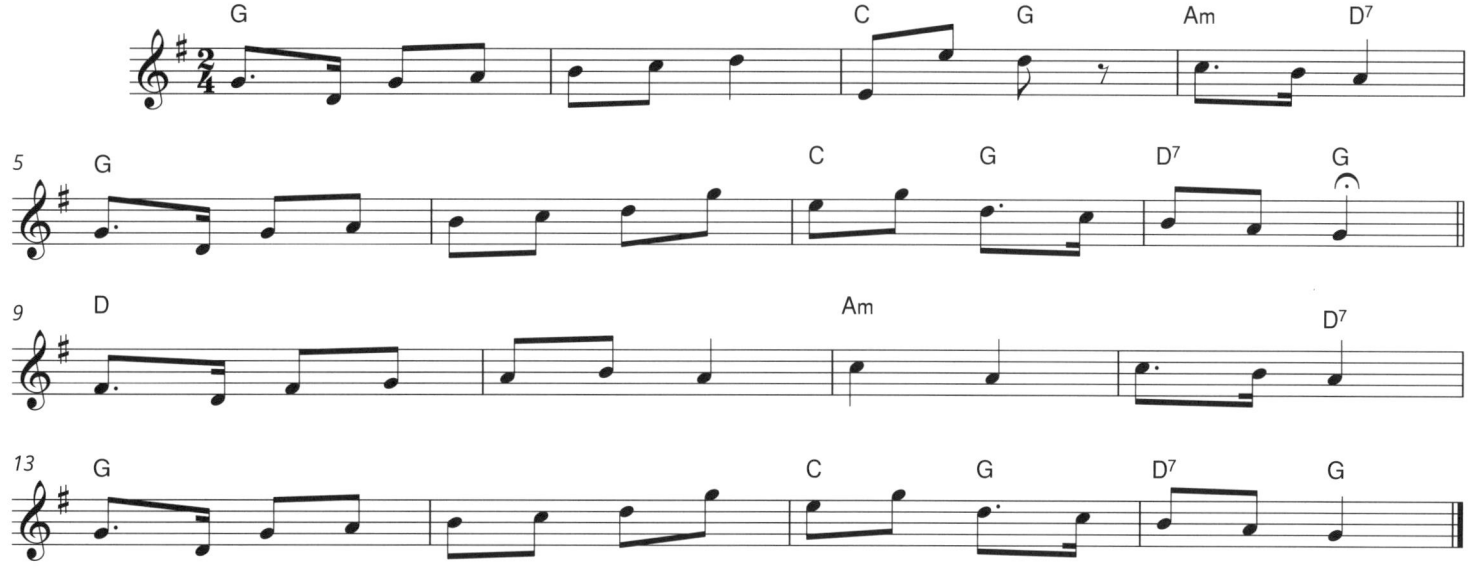

THE BASS STRATHSPEY
Composed by Corrina Hewat

Originally written in B♭ with the Highland pipes in mind, for the commission 'Making the Connection'; one of the first in the 'new voices' composer series in the Celtic Connections Festival.
It was recorded on *The Unusual Suspects* album, Live in Scotland.

CLAGGY JACKS

Composed by Margaret Watchorn

Goosegrass, cleavers and sticky-willy – the local name for the plant in north Northumberland is Claggy Jacks.
The rhythms of these names scramble through the tune, just as the plant climbs all over the hedgerow.
TT: Play this like a 3/2 hornpipe, it's definitely not a waltz...

THE BIRD MAN OF CHAMBERS STREET
Composed by Eilidh Steel

Bob McGowan is the curator of the Bird Collection at the National Museum of Scotland in Edinburgh and is also a keen fiddle player. A few years ago, his family commissioned me to compose this tune for his birthday.

DAWNS ELMO
(ELMO'S DANCE)
Composed by Cerys Hafana

I wrote this in the Hungarian mode (with the sharpened fourths), as an excuse to use the chromatic notes of the middle row of the triple harp more. In my head I can imagine it being played over and over again, getting repeatedly faster and more chaotic. (The Elmo of the title is in reference to St Elmo's Fire, the weather phenomenon, not Sesame Street).

DARK STACKS
Composed by Inge Thomson

A tune written for 'Da Fishing Hands' project. A moody dark tune written in lament for the drastic loss of kittiwakes due to sandeel overfishing in the 1980s. Happy to say since stricter fishing measures have been introduced, the sandeels have increased and kittiwake numbers are recuperating.
TT: we put this in the miscellaneous section as it's best played a wee bit faster than an air, and with a bit of a contemporary swing to it.

THE EGGSHELL BREWERY
Composed by Rachel Newton

The Eggshell Brewery was a folklore tale described in different cultures – a method of finding out if your baby was a changeling by distilling water from one eggshell to another until the baby stands and cries "I've been alive for hundreds of years and I've never seen the like!" In the unlikely event that this should happen, and the changeling is discovered, it would turn into a tiny old man with a wispy beard and disappear up the chimney in a puff of smoke. This tune is arranged for harp.

'DOLIG ABERTAWE
Composed by Angharad Jenkins

This tune was written after I returned home to Swansea during a Christmas break at Oxford Brookes University. My student digs were tiny; I couldn't play my fiddle without hitting the bedroom walls, so coming home to Gower and Mam's home-cooking provided a lovely creative time for me!
TT: Angharad's mam is Delyth Jenkins, who also has tunes in this book.

GOOD NEWS FOR PIGS
Composed by Helen Gentile

This 2-time bourrée was written during a camping trip on a Devonshire farm in 2020. I took inspiration from some of the farm's inhabitants. The pigs were fortunate enough to still be roaming the fields due to 'processing delays.' So, Good News for Pigs!

KINGFISHER ON THE CLUN
Composed by Ruth Angell

This is my most recent tune written after the emotional experience of first seeing a Kingfisher in the last few months. This piece was commissioned by Surge Forward music and arts.
(TT: Ruth plays this as a slow reel, but it works faster or slower).

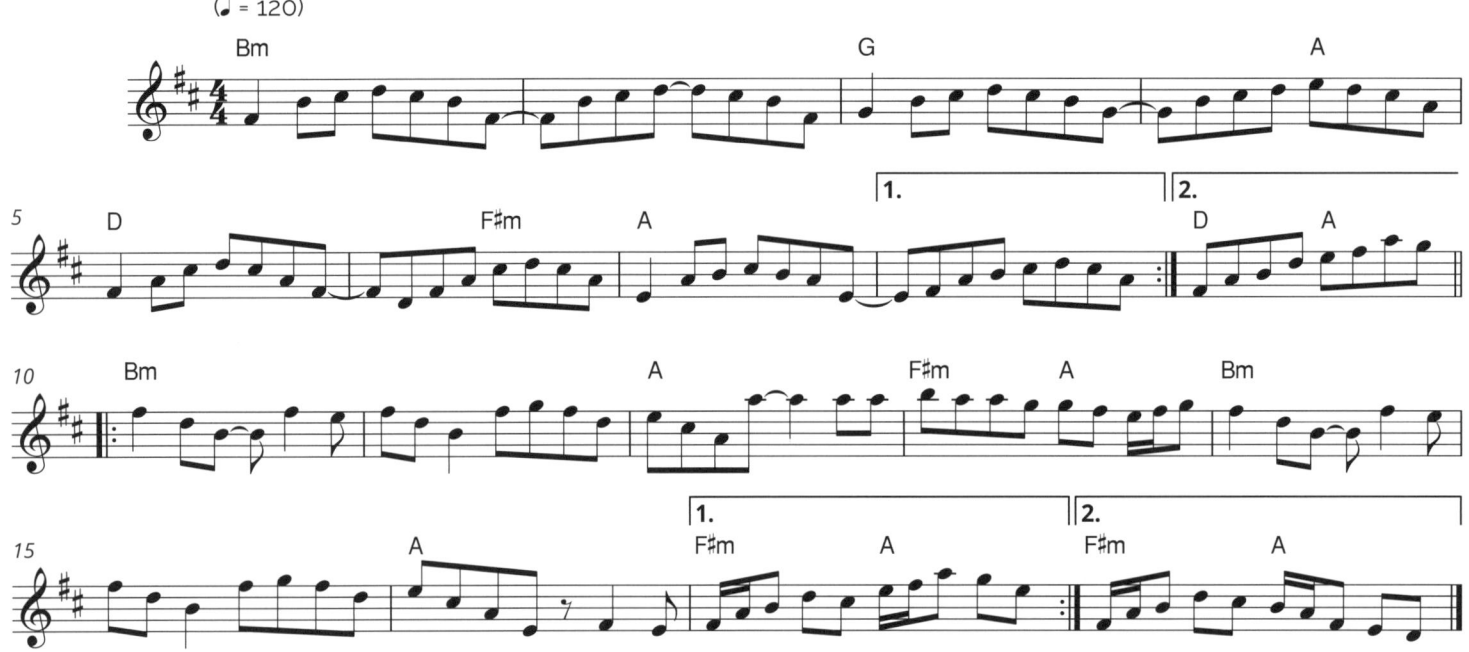

LEARN TO HAMBO!
Composed by Sophy Ball

I wrote this for my dad Dave Ball and his wife Fi Holliman after a folk camp in Germany. They repeatedly attempted to master the Hambo, and I wrote this to match the rhythm of the woman's steps. It wasn't a great tune with only those beats, so I added a few more and ended up with this little melody.

THE LIGHTHOUSE LOVERS
Composed by Karen Tweed

This bourrée was written for two astonishing musicians and dear friends, Nick Wiseman-Ellis and Fynn Titford-Mock. Their wedding took place in the Kleiner Preuße Lighthouse while the party/grand session was held in the local ice cream parlour. Yum!

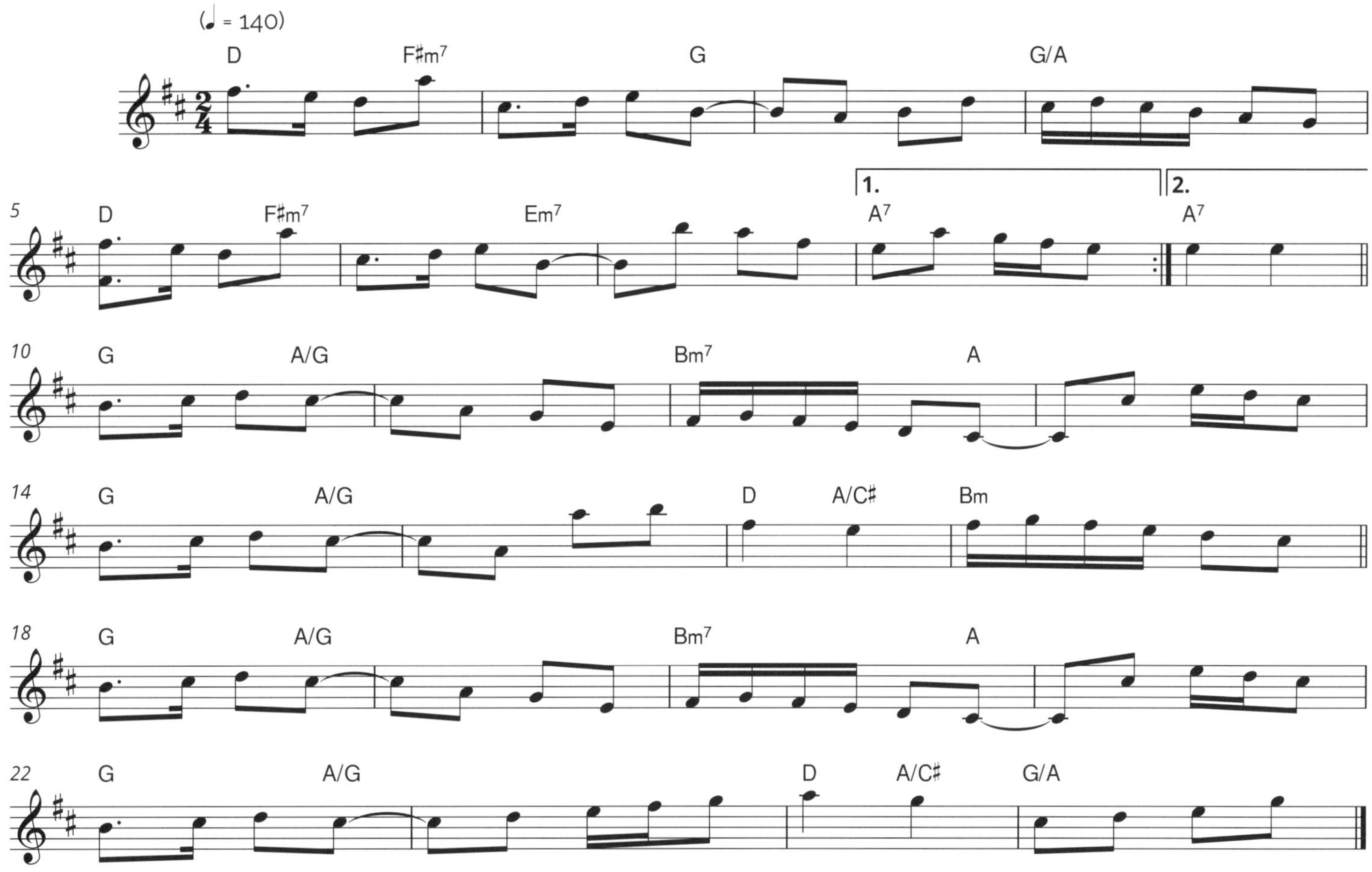

REVOKE ARTICLE 50
Composed by Isla Ratcliff

Written to channel my anger about Brexit...

MORAG'S WELCOME

Composed by Claire Gullan

A quirky rhythmical tune, in the style of a strathspey, written to welcome our new puppy Morag into our home. She is such a cheeky rascal!

ROTHBURY ROAD
Composed by Kathryn Tickell

For several years I lived in Northumberland's beautiful Coquet Valley and every road leading to the town of Rothbury has such spectacular views that I was often distracted from the driving. This tune, like the road, is best taken slowly. I wrote this on the Northumbrian pipes, but if I was playing it on my fiddle, I'd change the low G in bars 7 & 15 to an A and I'd definitely mess around with the 4th bar in the second half too… Interesting how different instruments send you in different directions, so feel free to experiment with this one!

SANDY MACDONALD OF SKYE
Composed by Gráinne Brady

'Sandy MacDonald of Skye' and 'The Great Exodus' are on my first album *The Road Across the Hills*.

SPRING AT LAST
Composed by Martha Woods

'Spring at Last' was written in April 2020, when Spring was one of the few things to be excited about.
The secret of this tune is that the A and B parts can be played at the same time!
*TT: We like this tune played in quite a lively way – almost like a 3/2 hornpipe, but it does work as a waltz too.
Martha is happy for people to play it however they want!*

TANTEEKA
Composed by Jo Freya

I wrote this specifically for a band called The Poozies. They were looking for Schottische style tunes at the time and I felt inspired to send them this. Happily, for me, they played and recorded it and Karen Tweed, part of The Poozies at that time, then taught it on various workshops and summer schools.

TUNE FOR A.LIEN
Composed by Catriona Macdonald

Written for Norwegian Hardanger fiddler Annbjørg Lien. One of my closest friends and musical sisters.
TT: Fiddle players – these bowings will help you get the right swing and groove for this tune. Catriona plays it faster than a waltz, and with the fiddle tuned AEAE which gives a great ring to the sound.

WELCOME JOY AND WELCOME SORROW

Composed by Jane Harbour

Titled with a line from Keats' 'A Song of Opposites', this tune is from Spiro's album *Welcome Joy and Welcome Sorrow*. The track rides the line between those extremes, like sunlight striking the surface of a deep body of water.

© 2015 Real World Works

airs

An air can cover a multitude of different types of tunes these days, but the ones in this section all lend themselves to being played slowly. They include laments, meditations and more, and they all give you the opportunity to still your mind and lose yourselves in the beauty of the melody and the act of playing music.

The timing can be an individual's choice – to pull the time around, playing rubato, pushing and pulling phrases as the player feels, adding ornamentation as the player wishes, to allow the piece to be a very personal expression. The women in this collection have a wealth of deep connection to the land, the people and the history which has gone before, and to the new and ever-shifting world which just never stops turning. We will always need to keep telling, sharing and connecting, and the airs in this collection give you just a taste of this.

Corrina Hewat

APRIL'S CHILD
Composed by Amy Thatcher

This tune was written for my very good friend and bandmate,
Lillias when she was pregnant with her first baby boy.

BRIGHT FIELD
Composed by Rowan Rheingans

I like to write tunes and songs out of lived experience. They tend to emerge after strong impressions –
whether that's of a place, a person, a conversation, or a journey. This particular tune was born after
a week of dancing in the wooden halls of farms in Sweden. It's about the moment the sun
hits your face again in the early morning and you're still dancing...
TT: Written for a fiddle with the bottom string tuned down to F# – we love the sound of the ringing strings.

Tuning: F# D A E

A TUNE FOR FRANKIE

Composed by Mairéad Ní Mhaonaigh

This air is based on a mantra that kept going around my head,
just like a prayer of notes to my late husband Frankie Kennedy.

DEORAÍOCHT AN T-SAIGHDIÚRA
(SOLDIER'S EXILE)

Composed by Niamh Ní Charra

I came up with the name for this lament after reading about the many Irish young men who fought in the American civil war. For some of those who fought, it was a way to become accepted in their new homeland, for others it was a place to train and garner support for the struggle back home in Ireland. The ferocity and length of the war was seriously underestimated, and since the Irish were frequently used on the front lines of both armies, they faced the prospect of fighting fellow Irishmen in a war that was not theirs. Some tried to leave and return to Ireland but were caught and charged with desertion. In America the punishment was to have the letter D branded on the soldier's forehead. For American deserters this meant lifelong shame, but for the Irish it meant instant and permanent exile from Ireland – should they have returned to Ireland, they would have been arrested immediately and charged with treason, a capital offence.

TT: We didn't put chords to this lament as it works so well as a solo piece, where you can really focus in on the melody, giving it lots of space to breathe and flow. However, if you'd like to add chords, or a drone, Niamh invites you to 'have at it!'

DON MacDONALD
Composed by Sue Harris

Our community band – Bandamania – has been going for 25 years and we've played for all sorts of local events and ceilidhs. Donny, one of our fiddlers was always there keen to play and be in the thick of it all. Sadly, he died in September 2018, leaving a gaping hole in our band. The best I could do was to write a piece in honour of him and his Scottish lineage.

I FEAR YOU JUST AS I FEAR GHOSTS
Composed by Jane Harbour

This tune is from Spiro's album *Lightbox*.
The track's slow rolling sound world burns with a raw mellifluous dolour.

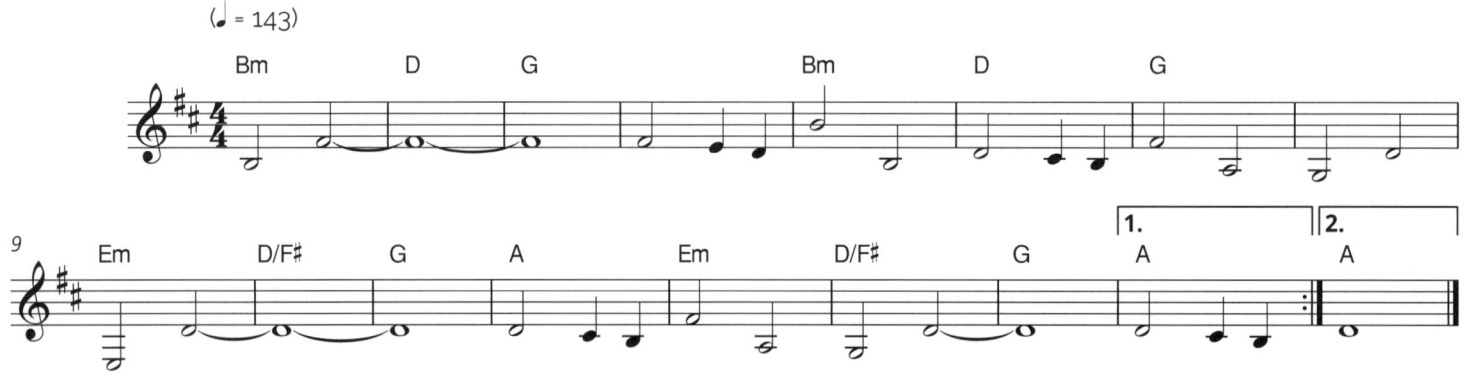

© 2009 Real World Works

IVAN'S

Composed by Ailie Robertson

Written to commemorate a wonderful friend, Ivan MacDonald of North Uist.

LAMENT FOR EMILY DAVISON
Composed by Susie Cochrane

I wrote this tune for Emily Wilding Davison when I was involved in a suffragette project in one of the schools I worked in. She is buried in Morpeth, Northumberland and her gravestone says, "deeds not words".

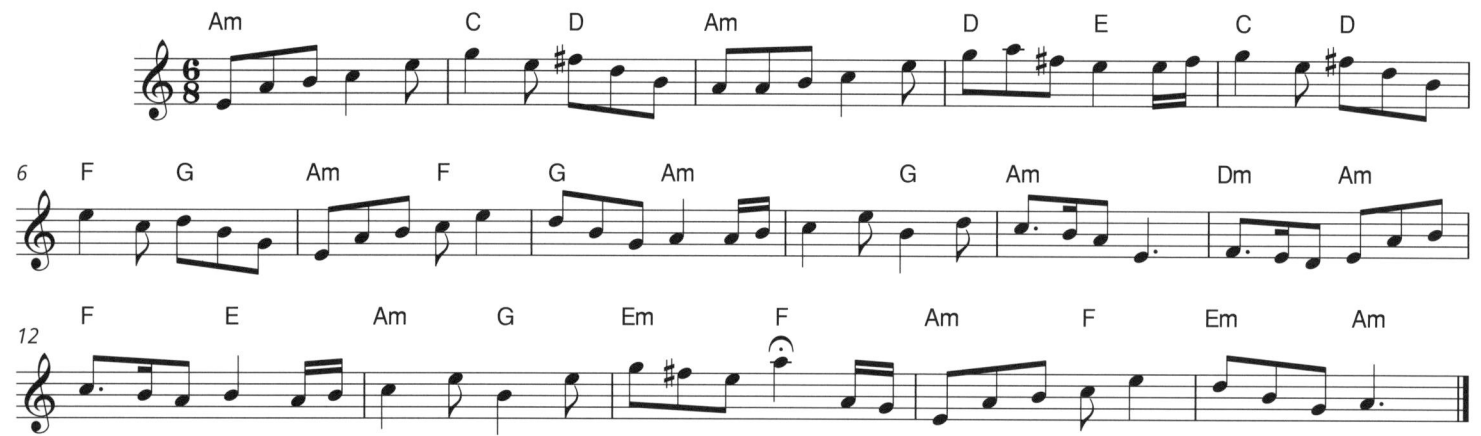

THE LEGACY
Composed by Cli Donnellan

A slow air, written in acknowledgment and presence of the legacy of ancestors.
TT: take this one slowly, giving it plenty of room to breathe… And enjoy those grace notes.

LLE ARALL
(ANOTHER PLACE)
Composed by Kate Strudwick

This slow air tries to capture the power of music to take you somewhere else, away from the noise.
It's dedicated to Margaret Rawling, my music teacher, who took time to encourage me – even if she was a bit fierce.

LLIDIART Y MYNYDD
(THE GATE TO THE MOUNTAIN)
Composed by Gwen Màiri

*Cyfansoddwyd yr alaw hon i fynd gyda darn o farddoniaeth gan fy hen dadcu, Thomas Jones, Gwarcoed.
Cyhoeddwyd y gerdd yn y llyfr 'Awen Myrddin (Llyfrau'r Dryw)', 1959.*
This tune was composed to go with a piece of poetry by my great grandfather, Thomas Jones, Gwarcoed.
The poem was published in the book 'Awen Myrddin (Llyfrau'r Dryw)', 1959.

MARRAM

Composed by Margaret Watchorn

I wrote 'Marram' for my husband Andy after a winter walk on the coast at Embleton, where marram grass binds the dunes together and the skies and sea are ever-changing. A/E drones are all the tune needs to complete it.

MAE'R GAEAF YN DYFOD

Composed by Branwen Mai Roberts

'Mae'r Gaeaf yn Dyfod', translates as 'The Winter is Coming'. I wrote this when I was 8 years old.
My harp teacher Eiddwen wrote it out for me. It is my first tune, but I am already composing more!

MAY THE ROAD RISE UP TO MEET YOU

Composed by Wendy Stewart

A setting of the old Irish blessing, with additional words reflecting how important a sense of belonging and security is to all of us. Written on a long bus journey round the west coast of Iceland in good musical company and stunning scenery, but with a longing to be back home.

RITA HUNTER OF AULTBEA
(RITA NIC AN T-SEALGAIR À ALLT-BEITHE)
Composed by Valerie Bryan

Written for my dear friend Rita Hunter, whose vital role in the development of Fèis Rois included creating intiatives such as The Cèilidh Trail and Ceòlraidh – projects which have become vital and integral to our traditional music life in Scotland.
TT: Several members of the Tunebook team have been to classes and workshops taught by Val. We're so glad to share her tune with you – it's a beauty.

SELKIE'S ECHO
Composed by Alison Jones

A deep-sea slow air this, inspired by beautiful Weston beach in East Devon – and the lovely mermaid I know who swims there.

STRETCHING HEART

Composed by Christine Edwards

Written in longing for Scotland, whilst over the Irish Sea.

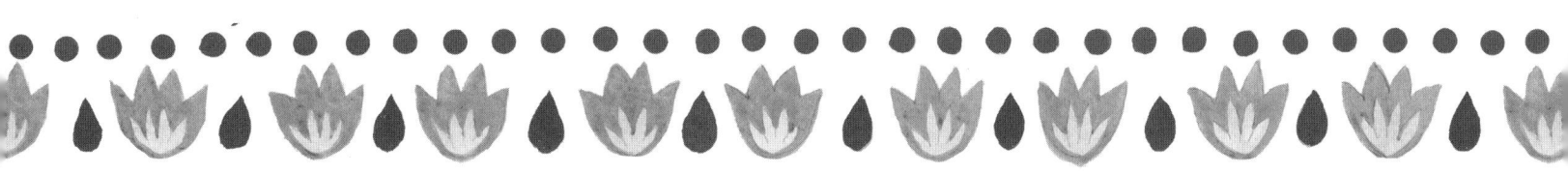

SUILVEN

Composed by Fiona Driver

'Suilven' is a slow air and my most requested tune. It was written when I was longing to climb the iconic mountain near Lochinver. When I eventually reached the summit, it was a magical experience, with pools of water scattered far below and clouds passing beneath me. This air has been played from Iceland to London, and was originally arranged for harp by Sarah Deere Jones. I also used it as part of my string quartet, 'Suite Assynt'.

THE COMPOSERS

FOLK TUNES FROM THE WOMEN
COMPOSER BIOGRAPHIES

 Sarah Allen is best known as a founder member of award-winning flute-based Anglo-Irish folk band, Flook. Flook have toured the world for over 25 years, invigorating the folk scene with their mix of traditional tunes and contemporary beats. Though originally classically trained, Sarah's first outings as a professional musician saw her playing alongside legendary free jazz drummer, John Stevens, whose approach to music challenged everything she had previously learned. Onwards from there, she joined ramshackle political big band, The Happy End, and then The Barely Works, another ground-breaking band on the UK folk scene. Sarah has played with Oysterband, Show of Hands, Sally Barker, Phil Cunningham and many others, and was a member of The Waterboys in their 'An Appointment with Mr Yeats' line-up.

www.flook.co.uk

 Ruth Angell is an English professional musician, composer, singer, songwriter and arranger. Growing up in Derbyshire she studied music at the Royal Birmingham Conservatoire and now lives in Shropshire with her husband and son. She has always loved folk music and has played the violin for 37 years. During her career to date Ruth has worked with some amazing musicians, including Rufus Wainwright, Terry Reid, Ashley Hutchings, Tony Kelsey, Spencer Cozens, Andrea Begley, Jim Moray and Joe Broughton to name a few. Music has taken her all over the world gigging from the UK and Ireland to Shanghai in China, Italy, Slovenia and many more places. Working with her husband, Sid Peacock, in Surge Orchestra, they run a music festival and have released three albums to date. As a duo Peacock Angell, they released the album *Love Forgiven* in 2011. On 03/02/23 Ruth released her debut solo album *Hlywing* to critical acclaim, "*A voice of immaculate beauty*" (Daily Mirror). Ruth's childhood in the hills of Derbyshire has been a strong influence on her work, and now being a mother and living in beautiful Shropshire she is still constantly inspired. As well as gigging in duos, bands and larger ensembles, Ruth has taught violin for over 20 years privately and in schools.

www.ruthangell.com

 Jess Arrowsmith is a traditional English fiddler and plays with Melrose Quartet, ceilidh band Hekety, in a duo with husband Richard and with Ian Robb as part of Arrowsmith: Robb Trio. Also a singer and songwriter, Jess has been composing traditional style tunes for well over 20 years. She dances Cotswold Morris and is a founder member of the side Pecsaetan. She has been artistic director for NYFTE (National Youth Folklore Troupe of England) since 2019.

www.arrowsmithmusic.co.uk

 Catrin Ashton is a musician, singer and dancer and has been performing English and Welsh traditional music for over 25 years in various bands, including The Outlandish Knights (ceilidh band), Treebeard and The Ashton Sisters. More recently she has been adding a hint of folk to Sheffield prog rock band, Haze. During lockdown Catrin worked on an album of original songs with Paul McMahon.

www.gabadon.co.uk

 Sophy Ball is a fiddle player from Derbyshire, brought up on a diet of ceilidhs, clog dancing and sessions, so dance music is really at the heart of what she does. Sophy loves playing tunes from anywhere in the world and sharing them with anyone and everyone who might like them too. She has played in the Pack, and with 422, The Bottle Bank Band more recently with the Andy May Trio and Alistair Anderson. She also runs several youth groups and loves teaching both fiddle and mixed instrument bands, working on arrangements and playing around with the tunes.

Helen Bell is a singer-songwriter, composer and violist. A finalist in the BBC Young Folk Award in 2000 with the trio Ola, she now runs a website which helps violists to access traditional music and publishes arrangements of traditional tunes as well as her own compositions. Her tunes almost always start life on the viola and are published on her website as alto clef sheet music for viola players (but she also provides treble clef transpositions for everyone else!)

www.helenbell.co.uk / www.folkviola.co.uk

 Mel Biggs is a Morris dancer, musician, visual artist and highly renowned melodeon tutor. She is a pioneer in the world of online folk music education with her online courses, classes and Patreon membership. During the pandemic, she also created 7 Days to Success – an online course for fellow tutors to help them grow their own online teaching business. In her professional career, Mel has risen from the EFDSS Aspire program with Andy Cutting to perform with Moirai (with Jo Freya and Sarah Matthews), and Boxtet (with Owen Woods, Ollie King and Matt Quinn). In 2021, Mel launched her sparkling debut solo album *From Darkness Comes Light*. The album, which portrays a journey through mental health and self discovery, is mostly original compositions which draw inspiration from English and European folk dance music. Mel has been involved in several recurrent Arts Council England funded projects including Jo Freya's Komposit Young Composers (with Annie Whitehead, Judith Weir CBE and Chris Woods), and cross-cultural theatre shows such as Priya Sundar's *Morris:Natyam*, Kate Flatt and Adriano Adewale's *The Oss & The Ox*, and Lisa Heywood's *Dance:Social*. She has also shared the actor-musician role of "Ann" in *Fisherman's Friends: The Musical* during its 2022/23 UK & Toronto tour.

www.melbiggsmusic.co.uk

 Pam Bishop plays duet concertina, leads the Mad Moll folk dance band and is music director of the Traditional Arts Team in Birmingham. Since the early 1960s she has been influential in getting people to participate in folk activities by organising music and song workshops and sessions, setting up and leading the Moseley Village Band, organising folk dances and tutoring at national concertina weekends. She has composed many tunes, band arrangements and accompaniments for songs and storytelling, and has been music editor for several songbooks. Pam became a resident singer and musician at the Grey Cock Folk Club in Birmingham in 1967, and helped to set up the women's group the Red Hens. In 1977, she joined the band Pigtown Fling which played for dances in Birmingham and also travelled in France. Interest in French music and dance led to another musical grouping known as Sabotage. After receiving several requests to play at women's events she set up the all-women dance band Cuckoo's Nest.

duetconcertina.wordpress.com

 Stacey Blythe is a composer, musician and multi-instrumentalist living and working in Wales. She was born in Birmingham and is a fluent Welsh speaker. She plays with Ffynnon vocal duo, Elfen, a trio with fiddle bass, harp and accordion and Gitân, a Celtic Indian duo with Rajesh David. She has toured the UK, Europe, America, Brazil and Australia She has also composed and performed with Adverse Camber on many storytelling theatre pieces.

www.ffynnon.org / www.gutan.co.uk

Imogen Bose-Ward is a fiddle player and singer-songwriter from Lanarkshire, Scotland, now living in Newcastle Upon Tyne. She completed Newcastle University's Folk and Traditional Music Degree in 2018 and since then has been gigging, recording and teaching. She has been writing and arranging with the folk quartet, Balter for a number of years, as well as with a jazz-inspired folk trio called The Cusp. She has recently been writing, playing and recording string parts for singer-songwriter Martin Longstaff aka 'The Lake Poets' as well as compiling her own solo material.

 Gráinne Brady comes from a musical household in Co. Cavan, Ireland. She grew up playing at traditional music festivals throughout Ireland, building from that a broad repertoire of tunes. Her fiddle playing style emanates from the musical lyricism of counties Cavan, Leitrim and Clare, and has more recently evolved to incorporate newfound Scottish influences. Now based out of Glasgow, Gráinne relishes in the creative milieu of the city's renowned traditional and folk scene, where players are writing new music, swapping tunes, and drawing from the rich cultural lode of shared regional styles and identity. Gráinne's second album *Newcomer*, released in 2021, features all of her own compositions and was inspired by the literature of Donegal writer Patrick MacGill.

 Valerie Bryan has always seen herself as a teacher and collaborator, rather than as a solo performer. However, she has over the years written a few tunes for people and occasions. Her musical background is broad and encompasses varied genres. Valerie grew up in Midlothian, singing by ear, often in harmony, with her family on walks and car journeys. Lessons in piano and flute led to making music with various choirs and orchestras, and then to study in Manchester. Her teaching career started in Edinburgh: here she played with various traditional musicians, as well as continuing more formal music-making. Valerie also spent several months busking in Germany. A move to Ullapool in 1985 as sole teacher of music in schools led to involvement with the Fèis movement, which gave her much joy as a tutor, learner, and editor, and great relationships with wonderful musicians. Since retirement, her musical activity has mainly been with large choirs, but she maintains a close connection with Fèisean.

 Chloë Bryce Fiddler and singer, Chloë Bryce, is an emerging talent in Scotland's folk scene. Brought up a Gaelic speaker in the North Highlands, her music is informed by a deep regard for the old tunes and songs embedded in Highland culture. Recently she has been uncovering music and stories linked to her local area and many of her compositions draw inspiration from this region. She has appeared on stages worldwide, performing at internationally renowned events including Festival Interceltique de Lorient, Celtic Colours International Festival, National Celtic Festival of Australia, Cambridge Folk Festival and Celtic Connections. She graduated from the Royal Conservatoire of Scotland in July 2020 with First Class Honours in Traditional Music Performance.

 Isla Callister is a Manx musician and Gaelic speaking fiddle player from the Isle of Man. Raised on the rich culture of the island, her sound reflects a strong connection to her native language, music and home. This blends seamlessly with influences from the prominent Irish session scene on the island, and her new home of Scotland. In 2016, she moved to Glasgow to study Traditional Music at the Royal Conservatoire of Scotland and soon after, joined 'TRIP'; a powerful six-piece band whose music spans the four corners of the Celtic diaspora. Isla, as part of a number of different line-ups, has performed across the UK and beyond at internationally acclaimed festivals such as Celtic Connections, Celtic Colours, Orkney Folk Festival, HebCelt and Festival Interceltique de Lorient. Last summer, she graduated with a First Class Honours in Traditional Music with an endorsement in Music Education and is now currently working on 'Creeaght', a composition, educational and performance project exploring the lives and experiences of women who have shaped the history of the Isle of Man.

www.islacallister.com

Mairéad Carey is an Irish traditional musician and composer from West Cork, and plays the fiddle, tin whistle, piano and flute. She has won numerous prizes at Fleadh Cheoil na hÉireann, among them three All-Ireland titles, including the Senior All-Ireland Flute Slow Airs title in 2014. She earned a first-class honours BA degree in Irish and Music (Joint Honours) from University College Cork, and a first-class honours Masters Degree in Ethnomusicology from UCC. She began her undergraduate career with a UCC Entrance Scholarship, and went on to achieve numerous scholarships, including the UCC Comhaltas Ceoltóirí Éireann award and a Quercus Creative and Performing Arts Scholarship. During her MA, she was awarded a Master's Excellence Scholarship, the Staf Gebruers Memorial Award in Music and the NUI Mansion House Fund Scholarship in Irish. She is currently a member of the National Folk Orchestra of Ireland. Mairéad is in great demand as a music tutor, having taught at Scoil Éigse at Fleadh Cheoil na hÉireann, Rauland Vinterfestival in Norway, Music on the Brain in Brittany, France, Féile Séamus Creagh in Newfoundland, Canada, and around her home county of Cork.

 Susie Cochrane has taught music in Northumberland and Newcastle schools for the past twenty years, latterly as Head of Music at Duchess' High School, Alnwick which has always had a strong reputation for its folk music groups. She gigs regularly with the ceilidh band Simply Northumbrian, and plays fiddle with the Borders Shetland Fiddle Group. She loves writing and arranging tunes for youngsters to play and is always inspired by the landscape around the Cheviots where she lives. In 2018–19 Susie lived and worked in Rome where she set up a ceilidh band and taught the Italian players tunes of the Northeast. The Italians, she discovered, love traditional music.

 Adèle Commins – Growing up in Co. Louth, Ireland, Adèle Commins developed a deep love of local heritage and of traditional music under the influence of her teacher Rory Kennedy. Playing both piano and piano accordion, she began composing at a young age, with many of her tunes inspired by the people and places around her, as well as her experiences of playing in local céilí bands. Adèle has performed internationally and is one of the musical directors of the award-winning Oriel Traditional Orchestra who have performed some of her arrangements and compositions. She is the Head of Department of Creative Arts, Media and Music at Dundalk Institute of Technology, Ireland and, as well as a performer, Adèle is a musicologist and has published in the areas of nineteenth and twentieth century Irish and English music and the scholarship of teaching and learning. She has also conducted research on musicians of the Oriel region. She released an album of new compositions entitled *A Louth Lilt* with Daithi Kearney in 2017. Further details on her compositions can be found at **www.alouthlilt.com**

 Zoë Conway combines a background steeped in Ireland's rich aural music tradition with a strong founding in classical music. She is a holder of the much-coveted All-Ireland Senior Fiddle Champion title, winning the prestigious competition in 2001. She was voted Best Traditional Female of the Year in Irish Music Magazine, Best Instrumentalist of the Year at the RTE Folk Awards, and she is also a featured musician on the current Leaving Certificate music syllabus in Ireland. Zoë has toured worldwide, performing in many prestigious concert halls including Carnegie Hall, New York, The Kremlin Palace, Moscow and The National Concert Hall, Dublin. She performs across a broad range of genres, from guest soloist with world renowned orchestras, to touring with Riverdance and working with mainstream international acts including Rodrigo y Gabriella, Damien Rice, Lisa Hannigan, Nick Cave and Lou Reed. As well as performing and composing Zoë has been active in commissioning other leading Irish composers with the aim of collectively presenting a snapshot of traditional Irish music alive today. She has released two solo albums and a live DVD as well as two albums with her husband, guitarist John McIntyre, a recording with two traditional music heavyweights, Máirtín O'Connor and Dónal Lunny, and a critically acclaimed album with Scots Gaelic singer, Julie Fowlis.

www.zoeconway.com

Rachel Cross grew up in Northumberland and the Scottish Borders and started learning penny whistle at the age of six, from her Dad, Arthur, followed by fiddle aged ten. She was lucky to be a part of the Small Hall Band, Kelso High School Celtic Group and Border Young Fiddles all of which made up most of her social life as well as her formamative musical experiencs. Rachel studied Folk and Traditional Music at Newcastle University and went on to play in several bands, as well being involved in lots of different music facilitation and teaching. In 2015 she moved to Bath to start a family and she is now embarking on new musical ventures in the South West, as well as continuing her work in music education, including leading the Bath Youth Folk Band.

www.rachelcrossmusic.wordpress.com

 Annette Davies plays accordion and fiddle. Her main musical interests are French, Breton and Welsh folk music. She is also a dancer and has been teaching French and Breton dancing for over 15 years. She was formerly very active in the Welsh folk dance and music scene but her introduction to folk music came through Morris dancing and attending English ceilidhs. Annette currently plays in a duo with Geoff Liles (guitar, fiddle, mandolin), and many of their tunes are composed by themselves. They are both members of Kantref – a five-piece band which plays mainly for French and Breton dancing but their repertoire also includes Welsh tunes, twmpath, ceilidh and concert tunes. Her compositions are strongly influenced by her love of dancing (though not all her tunes are dance tunes) and by having fun playing music with friends.

 Elsa Davies began to play folk music to make friends. She believes the music is friendship now and across time, a deep force of people's stories and lives and hope. She has been fortunate to learn from tradition bearers in Wales. She plays fiddle, crwth, piano and sings and is a freelance musician. Elsa's passion for connecting past voices with the present has inspired her to collect tunes and songs from archives all across Wales. This led to the project Deuair with Ceri Owen-Jones, two voices and fiddle and harp, which explores sound and place. Together they play with traditional Welsh idioms and instrumentation and make music for listening and dancing. Elsa composes, teaches and promotes folk arts in her community in Ceredigion, West Wales and she is always up for a good session.

 Cliodhna (Cli) Donnellan is an Irish traditional fiddle player, facilitator and producer from the small village of Mountshannon in East Clare. She founded and ran the Mountshannon Trad Festival for ten years (2010–2019). Cli hosted a weekly traditional Irish music radio show 'The Morning Dew' for Scariff Baby Community Radio 88.3 FM 92.7 FM from 2020-2022 and is an exponent of East Clare style fiddle playing. She describes her music style as that of an older era, deeply rooted and influenced by her native landscape. Cli produced and released her debut album *Beneath the Hedgerow* in October 2020. The album comes "highly recommended" by Irish Music Magazine stating that, "in a time where we have witnessed so much post-production in the studio, it's refreshing to hear an album that pares this back to the core." The album features two of her own compositions. In 2018, Cli concluded ten years study, part-time lecturing and coordinating position with the Irish World Academy of Music and Dance, University of Limerick with a Dr. of Philosophy. In 2021, she launched An Stábla project at her home, situated in the Slieve Aughty Mountain protected area of East Clare, overlooking Iniscealtra (Holy Island), providing a rustic setting for retreats and workshops while connecting with the surrounding landscape. It is an ideal haven for artists to spend time composing, writing or painting. Cli is currently composing new music, having received funding from the Arts Council of Ireland.

www.clieastclarefiddle.com

Marina Dodgson is a fiddle player from the North East of England. She is one of the directors of Phoenix Folk, a folk music company which promotes participation in traditional music both locally and online. Marina plays in the duo Miggins Fiddle with guitarist Maurice Condie. Together, they lead an extensive programme of online tune sessions and events, and their creative partnership forms the basis of several other bands and projects. This includes Frets 'n' Bows 'n' Tales 'n' Ales, a collaboration with Harry Gallagher (poet) and Cullercoats Brewery to create original tunes and poems to complement a range of beers inspired by stories of the Northumbrian coastline. Marina has published several collections of harmony parts for traditional tunes and she writes arrangements for the Phoenix Folk Virtual Ensemble and the Phoenix Chamber Folk Ensemble. Her work has been adopted into the repertoire of a number of ensembles, including the Tyneside Fiddle Alliance, and she was awarded first place in Composing Excellence at the 2021 Morpeth Northumbrian Gathering.

www.phoenixfolk.co.uk

 Fiona Driver is a musician, teacher and composer from Orkney. Her parents home-educated their children, first on the island of Hoy and then on the Orkney Mainland. They grew their own vegetables and raised animals for food. For many years they had no electricity or bathroom, and schoolwork was done by candlelight. Fiona taught herself to play at the age of 14 on her great grandfather Percy's old fiddle and started composing at 15. After playing and teaching throughout her 20s, She studied for a music degree, graduating in 2018. She plays classical music in local orchestras and played electric fiddle in a Western Swing band for 15 years. Now living in the Highlands, Fiona has many private fiddle pupils and has composed hundreds of tunes, many of which are played and recorded by musicians worldwide, including Saltfishforty, Troy MacGillivray and Shane Cook. As well as releasing several tune books and fiddle albums, Fiona was the first person to record an album of Orkney birdsong, and spends her spare time hiking, and climbing mountains.

www.fionadriver.com

 Christine Edwards grew up in Aberdeenshire and is an experienced performer, composer and teacher. She trained at the Royal Conservatoire of Scotland in both concert harp and Scottish harp. She studied Irish harp at the Royal Irish Academy of Music and Trinity College Dublin and holds a Licentiate of the London College of Music Diploma (LLCM) in Irish Traditional Music Performance. A dedicated teacher, Christine has set up various harp ensembles and teaches pupils all over the world through her online harp school.

 Tamsin Elliott is a multi-instrumentalist, composer and film-maker based in Bristol. Her roots are in the folk music of the British Isles, while her interests and playing styles extend to the folk music of France, Scandinavia and the Middle East as well as sound art and minimalism. Tamsin's debut solo album *FREY*, a set of pieces for accordion, harp, whistle and voice, accompanied by Sid Goldsmith's cittern and Rowan Rheingans' fiddle, was released to critical acclaim on Penny Fiddle Records in June 2022. In this work, Tamsin explores themes of limbo, pain, healing and acceptance, reflecting on the microcosm of her personal experience of chronic illness alongside wider themes of societal disconnection and environmental grief. She currently plays in the festival favourite Mediterranean fusion project Solana, European folk quintet Hedera, as well as in various traditional folk and ceilidh ensembles. Tamsin is currently collaborating with Egyptian oud player and composer Tarek Elazhary, exploring the parallels and idiosyncrasies between each of their folk traditions.

www.tamsinelliott.co.uk

Marit Fält is a multi-instrumentalist based in Scotland, brought up in Norway of Swedish parentage. She is best known as a Låtmandola player and is a leading proponent of using plucked instruments in a range of ways – equally as comfortable to lead as to accompany. After graduating from Newcastle University, she has recorded and toured with a range of acts, most recently with Marit and Rona, Tom Kitching and LYRE LYRE. In the last few years, she has gained a reputation for her work as a composer and has composed the soundtrack for three films together with Rona Wilkie, created the online free resource "The Scottish Composer" and released her debut solo album, *Irrationalities* in 2022, a self-composed work which highlights the topic of mental health.

 Marie Fielding – Edinburgh born, Marie is a fiddler and traditional music enthusiast, and has immersed herself in music from an early age, learning to play fiddle along to records in her bedroom age 10. Influenced by landscape and nature, her compositions also echo Gaelic song, pipe tunes, Cape Breton, Shetland and Irish culture as well as Indian patterns. She tries to tell stories with her performances, using texture and expression, mood and colour. Marie is presently Lecturer in Performance at The Royal Conservatoire of Scotland, and is a composer, producer, Tradmentor, storyteller and artist. She feels strongly about the message of self-belief and musical identity, especially to young female artists.

www.mariefieldingmusic.com / mariefielding.bandcamp.com

 Jo Freya has been a professional musician since her twenties and began playing publicly at the age of 13. She has been fortunate to be part of two revolutions on the folk scene; the first with The Old Swan Band specialising in English Country music from the South of the UK, in the 1970s, and then with the more outward looking, European perspective of Blowzabella in the 1980s. She writes tunes most often to fit a particular style of dance but also composes music that would not fit easily into a folk idiom. She is described as a maverick and 'mistress of reinvention' partly because she has been in many bands and enjoyed many collaborations with fellow artists in the UK as well as across Europe. Jo is also considered 'atypical' as a folk musician as her main instrument is soprano sax. She is self-taught and all her tone, decorations, vibrato and styles are informed by the sounds of folk instruments, their players and by folk song not by jazz tuition. She is a singer and songwriter too, working in various groups including Narthen and Moirai and singing in shows with Michael Morpurgo. She runs a young composer's project called 'Komposit' where young composers from any genre are placed in a workshop situation with an ensemble of mixed musicians from different music genres in order to enhance communication and broaden horizons. Jo has been appointed by the EFDSS as the new Artistic Director of the National Youth Folk Ensemble 2023–2025.

 Carolyn Francis is a professional fiddle and border bagpipe player based in Kendal, Cumbria. She is a founder of The Lakeland Fiddlers and has been a member of Striding Edge Ceilidh and Roots band since 1997. Carolyn writes tunes to mark significant events, people and places in the story of her life. She shares these with people who she teaches and performs with, and some have become locally very popular. She has been inspired by the many Lakeland fiddle manuscripts of old, and in 2002 moved from Lancaster to Cumbria and began writing her own tunes, usually whilst playing outside in the landscape.

www.striding-edge.org / www.facebook.com/LakelandFiddler1

Amy Geddes is a musician and educator and widely recognised as a leading light in the world of contemporary Scottish fiddle. Growing up in Galloway, Amy immersed herself in traditional music, song and dance, but has gone on to forge a career exploring musical genres whilst remaining true to her roots. Amy has now settled in Pathhead, Midlothian and is an active member of the Pathhead Music Collective with fourteen fellow local professional musicians. She plays fiddle and viola and sings. As well as composing for performance, Amy specialises in creating music for dance and works regularly with Slanjayvah Danza. She writes and arranges teaching materials and resources and released her first tutor book, *Fyne Fiddles Volume 1* in 2017. A book of original tunes is also on the horizon. Amy is also a regular live performer – solo, with Dean Owens' Whisky Hearts band and as one half of transatlantic folk duo Redwood Mountain. She also trains teachers across Scotland (with ABC Creative Music) and was nominated Tutor of the Year at the Trad Awards in 2015.

Catherine Geldard is a Shetland fiddler living and working in Newcastle upon Tyne. She has performed around the world with various bands, most notably Hjaltibonhoga with the Royal Edinburgh Military Tattoo and the band NE3Folk with whom she released an album. She has been writing tunes since school and gained a Masters Degree in composition and performance at university. She spends most of her time teaching and performing with bands varying from ceilidhs to contemporary folk music and even American rock, but you can often find her arranging tunes, writing tunes or working on commissions. The Shetland traditions that she was brought up with are a big influence in her writing, however she also includes elements from the music she is listening to at the time in her tunes, which range from simple lilting melodies to ferocious reels.

www.catherinegeldard.com

Karen Gledhill grew up in London and played piano and cello throughout her school years. She worked as a professional actress in theatre and television for 40 years and has taught music and piano to children and adults. She adapted 'A Midsummer Night's Dream' for primary school children, writing original music and lyrics that were accessible and enjoyable for them to perform. Karen now lives with her husband on a smallholding in Cornwall where she plays and writes music, and has converted a barn into a music studio for rehearsal and performance. She took up the accordion in 2013, and plays with the No. 1 Ladies Accordion Orchestra and the London Accordion Orchestra. She attended group classes with Paul Hutchinson at Cecil Sharp House for many years, and is a regular at Halsway Manor. She enjoys moving between the different disciplines of folk and orchestral playing and is writing original music for the accordion, absorbing multiple musical influences and making them her own. Her pieces are expressive and not generally in dance form, but they do tell stories and evoke moods.

Mairearad Green grew up on the West Coast Coigach peninsula of the Scottish Highlands, an area steeped in culture and local traditions and was introduced to folk music at an early age. Renowned for her deft and lyrical accordion style, as well as her dextrous piping, she is in great demand as a performer and composer. Often seen on stage alongside multi-instrumentalist Anna Massie, composer, Mike Vass, piping supergroup, Tryst, singer-songwriter, King Creosote and fiddler, Lauren MacColl. She has also previously toured with The Poozies, Karine Polwart, Box Club, and The Unusual Suspects. Mairearad is also a landscape painter, her work described as impressionistic, very much showcasing her emotional response to the landscape with which she is so familiar. Her latest limited-edition vinyl release *Hearth,* showcases Mairearad's two passions of art and music seamlessly combined.

www.mairearadgreen.co.uk

Helen Gentile is a clarinettist and multi-instrumentalist from Southampton. She developed a love of playing music for dance in her teens, having attended ceilidhs since childhood. During her studies, Helen lived in Brittany for a year, where she undertook an ethnographic research project exploring Breton folk music and dance. This year greatly influenced Helen's compositional style; many of her tunes draw on folk dance forms from Brittany and the wider balfolk scene across Europe. Helen's current musical projects include Threepenny Bit, Monkey See Monkey Do and a duo with fiddle player Lewis Wood, best known as the fiddle player from Granny's Attic.

www.threepennybit.com / www.thatmonkeyband.co.uk / www.gentileandwood.com

 Bryony Griffith is one of England's most highly regarded fiddle players and distinctive singers with a passion for delving through the tune and song manuscripts of her native Yorkshire. She has spent nearly 30 years playing for traditional dance and has extensive experience of devising innovative ways to present folk material for use in education. She is also a Senior lecturer on the Folk degree at Leeds Conservatoire. Her 2018 solo album of traditional English fiddle tunes, *Hover*, received 5-star reviews and award nominations including 'fROOTS Editor's album of the year' and Fatea Magazine 'Instrumentalist of the Year'. Bryony was a member of The Demon Barbers and The Witches of Elswick and still plays in the ceilidh band Bedlam, in a duo with husband Will Hampson, as a solo performer and more recently in a duo with Yorkshire musician Alice Jones. She also directs and arranges traditional songs for 4-part a cappella choir Shepley Singers.

www.bryonygriffith.com

 Claire Gullan is a broadcasting musician, music educator and podcaster living in Glasgow, Scotland. Originally from Aberdeenshire, Claire comes from a musical family – her grandfather played the fiddle for local ceilidhs and her father played the pipes. She was brought up playing in the Banchory Strathspey and Reel Society, then became a graduate of the Scottish Music Degree at the Royal Conservatoire of Scotland. She regularly enjoys playing for dances and ceilidhs. Claire has played fiddle on BBC Radio Scotland's legendary 'Take The Floor' programme with various Scottish dance bands. She is involved in a number of community projects throughout Scotland and online, as well as teaching music privately. She is the author of the fiddle tutor book, 'A Guide To Learning The Fiddle' and also enjoys composing and arranging music for a variety of situations. Claire loves promoting Scottish dance music, especially on her music podcast, 'Claire's Ceilidh'.

www.clairegullanmusic.co.uk

 Cerys Hafana is a composer and multi-instrumentalist who mangles, mutates, and transforms traditional music. She explores the creative possibilities and unique qualities of the triple harp, and is also interested in found sounds, archival materials and electronic processing. She comes from Machynlleth, Wales, where rivers and roads meet on the way to the sea. *Edyf* is her second album, released in 2022, and was selected as one of The Guardian's Top Ten folk albums of 2022. In January 2023, Cerys was also featured on Cerys Matthews' BBC 6 Music 'Highlights of 2022' New Year show.

Jane Harbour is a composer and musician living in Bristol, England. She is the driving force and main composer with Spiro, who she formed in 1993, playing violin and viola. She was classically trained in the Suzuki method and studied with Shinichi Suzuki in Japan, and became inspired by Bach, Bartók, Britten and Stravinsky. Her composition later became influenced by electronica, American minimalism and systems music. Spiro sprang from the folk session scene, its members sharing a love of traditional music. Jane quickly developed her trademark intricacy and interplay, featured on Spiro's seven releases on Real World Records, which Spiro have toured internationally. In 2017, her piece 'Kynde', a BBC Radio 3 commission for six voices, orchestra and archive recording, was performed live on Radio 3 by the BBC Concert Orchestra and the BBC Singers. Jane has also written for theatre, TV and live film and for other ensembles, including her leftfield pop 9-piece 'The Small Mammal Mirror'. Her latest composition is for Spiro and Synergy Vocals, due to record and tour soon.

www.janeharbour.com / www.spiromusic.com

Sue Harris started writing tunes regularly in the 1970s when she formed a women's Morris dance team on the Welsh borders and more dances were needed along with music for them. To that end she took up the melodeon to accompany the dancing. Her main instruments are hammered dulcimer and oboe, she plays the dulcimer in a ceilidh band, Polkaworks, and writes the odd tune for them. For some years Sue wrote music for theatre and radio plays and became involved in community projects, eventually settling into working mainly with Natural Voice choirs and community bands, mostly in Shropshire and Powys, mid-Wales. These have given her the opportunity to write all kinds of songs and lots of dance tunes.

Ernestine Healy hails from County Mayo and currently resides in Dublin. A qualified secondary school teacher, she has also worked as a lecturer and tutor in the Irish World Academy of Music and Dance, in the University of Limerick (2007–2010) and as a tutor in the School of Music at the University College Cork (2001–2008). An internationally recognized concertina player, as well as a tutor and producer on the Irish musical scene, Ernestine is a regular performer on both local and national radio, and has made numerous TV appearances, including 'The Fleadh Programme' and 'The Reel Deal' and was a featured performer on the concertina edition of Mná an Cheoil (Tg4 2016). Ernestine is also a well-known composer of traditional Irish music in Ireland, with compositions featured on numerous albums. She is widely sought after as a composer and arranger for ensembles and orchestras within the traditional music scene in Ireland. Working as the Executive Director of the 'Meitheal Residential Summer School' since its inauguration in 2004, she also acted as director of the 'Blas International Summer School for Traditional Music and Dance' (UL) from 2010–2016. Ernestine is currently Artistic Director for the Martin Donoghue Traditional Weekend.

www.ernestinehealy.com

Corrina Hewat is a maker, a composer, harper, singer, choir director and runs www.harpinscotland.com. Corrina was born in Edinburgh, but spent her formative years in the Highlands of Scotland which shaped her musical character; introvert, dark and slightly adrift. She is a passionate player, skilled collaborator and Scots Trad Music Awards winning tutor. She co-founded the big-band folk juggernaut The Unusual Suspects with David Milligan, and the female vocal/harp trio Shine and, since 2019, is a company director of Dragon Song Productions with Rachel Huggins, creating kids interactive musical theatre shows. She has written many commissions in the last two decades, 'Song of Oak and Ivy' being her next release. Corrina now lives in a small village in Midlothian with her family and her cats. She started writing music young, as a way of expression when she didn't have the words. She says, "I suppose I do that still."

www.corrinahewat.com

Angharad Jenkins is a fiddle player, songwriter and creative collaborator from Swansea. Described as "one of the dynamos of the Welsh folk scene", she's part of a new wave of musicians who are presenting the tradition in new and surprising ways. As a founding member of celebrated folk group Calan, she's toured extensively around the UK, Europe and North America. As a soloist, she's been involved in international collaborations as far as Korea and Australia. In 2021 she was commissioned to compose a piece of music for the National Youth Orchestra of Wales's 75th anniversary with her long-standing musical companion Patrick Rimes. She plays with her mother, the harpist Delyth Jenkins and with the Welsh 'supergroup' Pendevig. During her time with trac: Music Traditions Wales, she founded the youth residential courses Gwerin Gwallgo and Gwerin Iau. She's a proud member of Live Music Now, delivering accessible music workshops for children with special educational needs and early years. Her world changed after the birth of her children, taking her off on a new musical direction. She's fiercely determined to continue her musical career as a mother, and has recently been working on a body of work celebrating the joys and horrors of being a 'Mumsician.'

www.angharadjenkins.cymru

 Delyth Jenkins began her musical career in the 1970s with the Swansea-based folk group Cromlech, before going on to form the innovative instrumental trio Aberjaber with Pete Stacey and Stevie Wishart. In addition to sustaining a solo career, she has also composed and performed music for numerous theatre productions, including 'Under Milk Wood', and an adaptation of George Borrow's 'Wild Wales'. She has collaborated with poets, storytellers and dancers. She particularly enjoys her collaboration with her daughter, fiddle player Angharad Jenkins, together often known by their initials DnA. They have two albums to date and have published a DnA Tune Book. In addition to the albums that she has made with various groups, Delyth has also released four solo albums and has published several collections of her own compositions and arrangements of traditional Welsh tunes. Her book 'That Would be Telyn' (pub. Y Lolfa) tells the story of her remarkable 186-mile walk along the Pembrokeshire Coast Path, when she took with her a small harp and gave a series of impromptu path-side concerts along the way.

www.delyth-jenkins.co.uk / www.dna-folk.co.uk

 Angharad Jones is an instrumentalist and composer of dance tunes who has accompanied many of the winning dance groups at the National Eisteddfod of Wales. She has been a computer analyst, a university lecturer, a student of the clarinet at the Welsh College of Music, a conductor of a choir and mother of a daughter in an indie/folk band. She composes all her best tunes whilst sat in the car at traffic lights and describes herself as a Doctor Who companion in waiting. She used to be a lecturer, but regenerated as a music teacher and organiser of Welsh tune workshops in South Wales and says she will continue to compose until the Tardis and The Doctor come calling.

 Alison Jones was born in Swansea, and after plenty of travelling made her home in beautiful Devon. She's played music all her life, touring widely with the Barely Works and other lovely bands before setting up her band of many years now, Spin 2. She teaches fiddle and runs a community folk band, Newtown Roots Band which mixes interesting arrangements with traditional tunes. She also enjoys taking part in a variety of tune sessions that run in and around Exeter. Alison loves writing tunes – the excitement of finding a little idea that pleases her, then playing with it and following its thread through to a finished piece of music. Sometimes she's inspired by the stunning landscapes of sea and moor that surround her; sometimes by events; sometimes by the people she loves. It's a special feeling to know that a tune she's written takes on a life of its own when it goes on to be played by other people.

Instagram: @alijonesfiddle / www.spin2.co.uk

Lauren MacColl is considered one of Scotland's most expressive fiddle players. From the Black Isle, she studied music in Glasgow before returning home to the Highlands where she draws much of her musical inspiration. A founder member of both chamber-folk quartet RANT and song-trio Salt House, Lauren also performs with Rachel Newton in Heal & Harrow and is in demand as a session musician on both fiddle and viola. In 2017 she was commissioned by Fèis Rois to write a suite of music based on the life and prophecies of the Brahan Seer. Premiered at Celtic Connections, the music was released as an album to critical acclaim. Her latest commission 'An Ear | East' was inspired by coastal tales from around the Moray Firth. Lauren released a book of her own tunes 'To the North...' in 2019. In addition to performing and writing, Lauren has run the Black Isle Fiddle Weekend for a decade and teaches regularly at summer schools and locally with community groups.

www.laurenmaccoll.co.uk

 Catriona Macdonald is a Shetland fiddler, composer and scholar. In addition to playing in her own band, she was a founder member of Blazin' Fiddles, and currently plays with the fiddle band String Sisters. Catriona is the Degree Programme Director for the BA in Folk and Traditional Music based at Newcastle University and is in the final stages of her creative practice doctoral thesis which aims to recover and respond to women's roles within pre-20th century vernacular cultural practices in Shetland.

 Louise Mackenzie is from Nigg in Easter Ross and as a youngster, was taught by three of Scotland's most respected and treasured Tradition bearers; Aonghas Grant, Alasdair Fraser and the late Dr Tom Anderson. She was greatly inspired and influenced by her mentors and inherited a love for both teaching and composing. She regularly teaches for Fèis Rois and has been involved with various Fèisean for over 35 years. She was also a full-time Strings Instructor in East Sutherland for 15 years. In 2020, Louise was nominated as Tutor of the Year in the MG Alba Scots Trad Music Awards.

 Mary Macmaster is probably best known for her work with the metal-strung clarsach and the fantastic Camac electro-harp. She sings in both Gaelic and English language. During the last thirty years Mary has toured throughout the world with Sileas (with Patsy Seddon); The Poozies (with Patsy Seddon, Karen Tweed, Sally Barker, Kate Rusby, Eilidh Shaw, Mairearad Green, Sarah McFadyen and Tia Files); Shine (with Alyth McCormack and Corrina Hewat); and with Donald Hay, a brilliant percussionist. For the past few years she has also been part of the organisation running the annual Edinburgh International Harp Festival. She has toured with Dogstar Theatre Company in a production of Hamish MacDonald's 'Seven Ages of Man', with Licketyspit's wonderful children's adventure tale 'Molly Whuppie' and with Grid Iron Theatre Company's 'The Devil's Larder'. She has collaborated live and in the studio with many wonderful musicians including Scottish hero Dick Gaughan, Northumbrian pipe virtuoso Kathryn Tickell, English folk legends Norma Waterson and Jo Freya, and Sting.

 Breesha Maddrell is a flute and whistle player and singer from the Isle of Man. She has played with Skeeal and Moot and has performed throughout Europe and in the USA and features on numerous recordings. She currently sings and plays with musical magpies, Clash Vooar, and with Manx Gaelic choir, Caarjyn Cooidjagh. In her spare time, she is Director of Culture Vannin, an agency promoting, supporting and developing Manx culture.

Gwen Màiri grew up in a Welsh-speaking home in Scotland and studied at the RSAMD. Her first solo album, *Mentro*, was released in 2019 and explored her Welsh and Scottish heritage through traditional and original tunes and poetry. Her playing can also be heard on the albums of Gwilym Bowen Rhys, *O Groth y Ddaear*, (2016), *Arenig*, (2019) and *10 Mewn Bws* (2013). Gwen is involved in the work of the Clàrsach Society and was the clàrsach instructor at Sgoil Ghàidhlig Ghlaschu for many years as well as the pedal harp tutor for the junior department of the Royal Conservatoire of Scotland. She enjoys performing with professional orchestras, tutoring the Welsh youth folk ensemble, Avanc, and publishing books of music for lever harp through Alaw. She has represented Wales at the Festival Interceltique de Lorient and her work includes a songwriting commission from the National Library of Wales and a project with Cardiff-based theatre company, August 012, exploring the Welsh vocal tradition of Canu Pwnc. Her album *Douze Noëls* was released in 2021.

 Anna Massie is equally at home as an accompanist or melody player, and is one of Scotland's foremost guitarists. As well as being a skilled multi-instrumentalist renowned for her work with Blazin' Fiddles, RANT and Mairearad Green, she also presents BBC Radio Scotland's flagship weekly traditional music programme, *Travelling Folk*. Three-time nominee for Best Instrumentalist at the Scots Trad Music Awards, 2021 winner of the Trad Music in the Media award for her *Black Isle Correspondent* work and 2022 Producer of the Year award, Anna is a highly talented musician, presenter and producer.

 Maeve McCann is an accomplished folk musician, composer, scientist and writer from Ireland. She plays Whistle, Uilleann pipes and Bodhran. Maeve has played music since the age of 6, enjoying the freedom, fun and possibilities that come with playing folk music. She grew up steeped in the music of Fermanagh and surrounds, with an ear for both the beauty in traditional and innovative music. Composing has become a means of expression and exploration by which she interprets the world. She has performed locally and internationally as a solo artist and is a founding member of the band Na Cailligh.

nacailligh.com / soundcloud.com/maevemccann

 Rebecca McCarthy Kent is a multi-instrumentalist, equally accomplished in both classical and traditional music. She has won multiple Fleadh Ceoil All-Ireland titles in both fiddle and piano and was 2019's Bonn Óir Seán Ó Riada Fiddle Champion. She has toured nationally and internationally with different musical groups in Germany, Canada, USA, Dubai, Romania, China and is a member of the traditional band '3 on the Bund.' Rebecca is a qualified primary school teacher and has achieved first place in the TTCT teaching diploma in Irish music. She has taught as fiddle and grúpa cheoil tutor for Tramore Comhaltas Branch as well as tutoring at the Pat Kelly Irish Music School in Germany for 9 years and has tutored at many other workshops and festivals around Ireland including Scoil Éigse, Meitheal Summer School, Kincora Trad Fest and Coalisland Trad Fest, to name but a few. Rebecca also achieved a First Class Honours for her master's degree in Irish Music Performance at the University of Limerick.

 Sarah McFadyen is originally from Hoy in Orkney, presently living in Midlothian. She plays fiddle, 5 string banjo and sings. Sarah's main band of recent times is The Poozies, playing alongside Mary Macmaster on harp, Eilidh Shaw on fiddle and Mike Bryan on guitar. Over the years she has played and collaborated in many musical bands and projects, including Sandy Wright & The Toxic Cowboys, Aberfeldy, Harem Scarem, Dance Bandits, The Fiddletree Collective and Oceanallover. As well as being a musician, Sarah is also a maker and visual artist. Much of her world is immersed in making paintings. She writes poetry which informs the paintings, and sometimes these poems become songs. She has also made two fiddles to date. Sarah is passionate about the power of creativity and believes that all her creations from different disciplines work to support and inform each other.

www.sarahmcfadyen.com

Kirstie McLanaghan is a self-employed fiddle teacher and musician based in Edinburgh, teaching on a one-to-one basis and also for Scots Music Group and the Adult education project within Edinburgh Council. She graduated with First Class Honours in Applied Music from the University of the Highlands & Islands last year. During her time on the course, she studied (amongst other things) composition. She found that she really enjoyed composing and has since written many tunes, often as gifts for people. Kirstie's world changed on the 15th May 2021 when her son Lewis took his own life. He was 20 years young and a gentle soul with kindness running through him. She now finds herself in a world that she didn't know existed, and sadly there are so many other people living there too. Kirstie says, "People are scared to use the word suicide, but it needs to be used if we are to break the stigma attached to it."

Rachael McShane is a singer, cellist, fiddle and viola player based in the North East of England, best known as an original member of English folk big band, Bellowhead. She also tours with her own band Rachael McShane & The Cartographers alongside Ian Stephenson and Julian Sutton. Their "distinctive and captivating" debut album, *When All Is Still* was released on Topic Records in 2018. As well as performing, Rachael is a teacher and workshop leader, working in schools teaching strings, ensembles and choirs and running online fiddle courses for adults. She has also been a part of educational projects with organisations such as Aldeburgh Young Musicians and the National Youth Orchestra.

www.rachaelmcshane.co.uk

Mari Morgan is a south Walian living in north Wales, often found playing instruments (mostly the ffidil/violin) singing, dancing and doing different creative things with all sorts of people. This includes bands and projects with schools and the community. She comes from a varied musical background having played with folk, classical and pop outfits. Her love of playing Welsh tunes started when accompanying her uncle's Welsh folk dancing group. She also loves to play instruments, sing and dance with her daughter, Nyfain.

Rachel Newton is a singer and harpist who draws on poems and ballads that are hundreds of years old, working them into her contemporary compositional style to create a rich sound that is ambitious, original and unique. A skilled collaborator, Rachel is a founder member of The Shee, The Furrow Collective and the Lost Words: Spell Songs, she also has a duo project, Heal & Harrow with Lauren MacColl. Rachel was awarded Musician of the Year at both the Scots Trad Music Awards and the BBC Radio 2 Folk Awards. Her albums *To The Awe* and *Here's My Heart Come Take It* were shortlisted in the Scottish Album of the Year (SAY) Award. She was awarded a Critics Award for Theatre in Scotland (CATS) for Best Music and Sound. Co-founder of The Bit Collective, a group focusing on equality and diversity in folk and traditional music, Rachel has organised various campaigns and events, including the Trad. Reclaimed: Women in Folk festival at Kings Place, London in 2019.

Niamh Ní Charra is a musician, composer and professional archivist. Strongly influenced by a wealth of local Sliabh Luachra musicians, she is a multiple award winner on both fiddle and concertina, and toured from 1998 to 2006 as a soloist with Riverdance, before returning to Ireland where she is now based. Her 5th album, *Donnelly's Arm*, recorded during the Covid-19 pandemic, was crowned Number 1 Trad Album of 2021 by Alex Monaghan, reviewer for several publications including Irish Music Magazine, Living Tradition and FolkWorld. She is the recipient of several other awards including 'Instrumental Album of the Year' in 2014 in the Chicago Irish American News' TIR awards for her previous album *Cuz*, and 'Female Musician of the Year' in 2012 and 2014 in the Live Ireland Music Awards. Her music also featured on the programme 'Ireland in Song' which aired on Aer Lingus transatlantic flights. Along with touring extensively as a solo artist and with her own band, Niamh has also performed and recorded with The Chieftains, Galician piper Carlos Núñez, and Basque musicians Ibon Koteron and Xabi Aburruzaga. She regularly gives workshops and masterclasses on both fiddle and concertina, has performed for several presidents and members of royalty, and has coordinated concerts on behalf of the Irish government. Her work in both the music and archive professions was recently recognised when she was elected to the Irish Traditional Music Archive's board and a selection of her compositions featured in their *Saothar* series in July 2022.

www.niamhnicharra.com

 Éadaoin Ní Mhaicín is an award-winning multi-instrumentalist and composer from County Mayo specialising in Irish folk music traditions. She has received many accolades throughout the years including the 2022 Arts Council Ireland Next Generation Artists Award, multiple All-Ireland Fleadh Cheoil titles, The Camac Trophy Award at Lorient Interceltique Festival, Milwaukee Irish Festival and Irish World Academy Partnership Award and is a two-time Oireachtas na Gaeilge champion. Éadaoin graduated with a First Class Master's degree in Irish Music from The University of Limerick in 2019. She also holds a High Achievers Senior Certificate Award in Classical Violin from the RIAM and has a TTCT teaching diploma in Irish music. In 2020 she released her first single with EADAOIN, which featured at number one in the iTunes World Charts in Ireland. In early 2023 she will be releasing a debut EP with LÉDA, a two-piece folk band which has recently completed an Irish & UK tour. Éadaoin has collaborated with internationally renowned artists across a diverse array of genres and performed on stages across the globe such as Croke Park, Broadway, RDS, Broadway, National Concert Hall and The Barbican Theatre in London to name but a few. Her music has taken her to China, Kazakhstan, New Zealand, mainland Europe, Canada, North America and frequently to Áras an Uachtaráin to perform at the invitation of President Michael D Higgins. Éadaoin is currently working on her debut solo album which will be due for release at the end of 2023.

 Mairéad Ní Mhaonaigh is a fiddle player and sean-nós singer from the Gaeltacht of Gaoth Dobhair in County Donegal and is passionate about preserving the traditional music from her area. She is also a composer and has been commissioned to write music for various projects over the years. She is a founding member of the renowned traditional music group, Altan. For over thirty years she has toured the world with Altan, travelling all over Ireland, the United Kingdom, Europe, Australia, New Zealand, Asia and the USA. She has played in venues as diverse as The Albert Hall in London, The Sydney Opera House and The Hollywood Bowl. Mairéad has made one solo album in 2009 called *Imeall*, and is also a member of other ensembles such as; String Sisters , comprising of female fiddle players from all over the world, SiFiddlers a Donegal based group of female fiddlers focusing on the rich Donegal tradition, her family band, Na Mooneys and T with the Maggies along with Moya Brennan, Maighread and Triona Ní Dhomhnaill. Mairéad was awarded 'Donegal Person of the Year' in 2009 by the Donegal Association in Dublin for her work in promoting the County and its rich culture worldwide and in 2017 was awarded TG4 Musician of the Year.

Sarah Northcott is a fiddler, composer, music teacher, community worker, project manager and proofreader living in Tweedsmuir in the western Scottish Borders. Originally from the south of England, she's lived in Scotland since 1989. She plays for dancing with The Robert Fish Band, The Little Biggar Band and in an occasional trio with Matt Smith and Duggi Caird. Sarah has worked in a variety of community projects and charities, from HIV/AIDS support to community music projects with Scots Music Group (SMG) and others, including projects involving those who have experienced homelessness and mental health issues. She is currently the Development Worker at SMG and teaches mixed instrument classes there. She writes tunes for both love and money!

www.hartreemusic.co.uk

Mirain Owen submitted her tunes for this book when she was 16 years old and playing Welsh traditional music in sessions in Swansea! As a "crazy feminist" according to the boys at school, she thinks it's brilliant to see female musicians being brought to light and is studying Welsh, Psychology and Politics.

Harriet Power is a melodeon player and one half of the duo Shivelight. She studied music and ethnomusicology at Royal Holloway, before discovering the music of Chris Wood and Andy Cutting and picking up the melodeon. With Shivelight, she plays a mixture of self-penned, traditional and contemporary European dance tunes.

Isla Ratcliff is a Scottish fiddle player, singer and composer from Edinburgh, with a background in classical violin and piano. She has a deep interest in tradition, cultural politics, the environment, and the positive impact music has on our wellbeing. Her debut album, *The Castalia* (2021), features traditional and self-composed tunes inspired by the four months that she spent in Cape Breton, Nova Scotia in 2019, including a trip to New Brunswick to meet her distant relatives. Described as 'quite the best debut album that has come this way in a long time' (*The Living Tradition*), her album expresses her love for the tradition, its ethos of community, and the power of music to bring people together. Isla has performed at Celtic Connections, Cambridge Folk Festival, Sidmouth FolkWeek, the Edinburgh Festival Fringe and the BBC Proms. She graduated with an MMus Scottish Music degree from the Royal Conservatoire of Scotland in 2020, and with a BA Music degree from Oxford University in 2017. Aged 13, she played a trad duet with Nicola Benedetti in Edinburgh's Usher Hall.

Helina Rees is a freelance musician who discovered the joy of folk playing and writing years after learning via the classical route. After graduating from the Royal Academy in London (1996), she began working in and outside of studios with several extremely talented non-classical musicians, including Ryland Teifi, Rob Reed, Mick Lister, Christian Phillips and Climbing Trees. She ran a string quartet for commercial work where she had several opportunities to arrange for strings in various styles. Helina was a member and busy performer of the Welsh folk band Elfen (once finalists in the Lorient Festival Trophee Loic Raison), with whom she enjoyed co-writing, co-arranging and performing at several venues in the UK. She recorded two EPs and the album *March Glas*. She has also enjoyed working with successful commercial bands (e.g. Disturbed, Illegal Eagles and The Carpenters Story) in performances. Her love for bluegrass grew after an experience at the 'Sore Fingers' course one summer where tutors from Texas and Nashville blew her away. She now teaches folk fiddle as well as conventional violin and piano.

Patsy Reid is a musician, composer and teacher specialising in Scottish traditional music and based in Perth, Scotland. She mostly plays fiddle and viola and is a busy session player, having played and recorded with the who's who of UK folk music. Patsy recently formed a new band called LYRE LYRE with Alice Allen and Marit Falt and launched a new album at Celtic Connections 2022. Celtic Connections also commissioned her to write her first extensive piece of music, 'Bridging the Gap', which was recorded and released on Vertical Records in 2008. Since then, she has released a further three solo albums, appeared on countless others and written many more tunes and larger pieces of music. In the last couple of years, she's written and arranged for The Grit Orchestra and Tryst.

 Rowan Rheingans is a fiddle player, banjoist, songwriter and theatre-maker. She composes and performs with bands Lady Maisery and The Rheingans Sisters and was part of the 10 piece super-group called Songs of Separation. With these acts, she won two BBC Radio 2 Folk Awards and is a six-times nominee. Her debut theatre show 'Dispatches on the Red Dress', co-written with Liam Hurley, premiered at 2019's Edinburgh Fringe and won a Fringe First Award for New Writing. Rowan's greatest joy is social music and dance. She loves being a professional folk musician and conjuring music for an audience, but thinks the heart of this music is the social gathering. She is continually inspired by the idea of tunes being passed like coins between generations of peoples and of a changing and evolving musical tradition. Rowan says, "I find there is so much room for experimentation and play within the soft boundaries of traditional music and I love that I'll never run out of traditional musics from different parts of the world to become interested in and enchanted by!"

rowanrheingans.co.uk

 Bethan Rhiannon sings in both English and Welsh and is also winner of the national clog dance competition in Wales. She learnt her dancing from her father who was also a champion dancer. She has appeared as a music commentator on radio and television and developed and delivered music and dance workshops for young people throughout Wales.

www.calan-band.com / www.instagram.com/bouufff_folkhero/

 Llio Rhydderch is a triple harper from Anglesey, North Wales. At Llio's touch, the Welsh triple harp is a meeting point of tradition and creativity and two Welsh harp lineages that extend back many centuries. Raised in a living tradition, music has been a constant in Llio's life, shared around the family hearth from her earliest memories. Her creative explorations and boundary-breaking artistry have taken traditional Welsh music and the triple harp to soundworlds of exquisite vision and emotional depth. Celebrated around the world through her recordings and international performances, Llio's monumental contribution to Welsh culture was finally recognized with an Honorary Fellowship from Bangor University in 2018.

 Lucy Rivers is a Welsh singer, fiddle player, composer, actor and theatre maker and is co-founder of the award-winning gig-theatre company Gagglebabble. Lucy has performed with a number of bands and played on many recordings over the years, including Os Sambistas, Rachel Taylor-Beales, VOW, Hopeless Sinners, Spirit of Nimba, and has made three albums with her Welsh folk duo Olion Byw. She has performed at many festivals including Lorient, Mosley, Gower, Edinburgh Fringe, Latitude, Galway, Brighton Fringe, Folk Alliance and has collaborated with folk musicians in West Bengal. She works extensively in Theatre and radio as a composer, lyricist and performer touring nationally and internationally, and likes to push the boundaries of music theatre. She has also directed two Welsh music tours called *Cylch Canu /Song Chain*, and has led workshops for youth folk ensemble Avanc.

lucyrivers.co.uk / gagglebabble.co.uk

Ailie Robertson is a musician in the broadest sense: composer, arranger, teacher, improviser and harp virtuoso. Awarded LiveIreland's 'Female Musician of the Year 2019', her synthesis of Scottish, Irish and contemporary harping technique into an individual style represents the realisation of "otherwise unimagined possibilities for the Celtic harp". She won the award for 'Innovation in Traditional Music' in the 2019 Scottish Awards for New Music and her with her band, The Outside Track, she has performed all around globe, has published six volumes of harp music which are used by students around the world, and has taught at harp festivals in Europe, Canada, the USA, Australia and Asia.

 Margaret Robertson is originally from Shetland and was taught by Dr Tom Anderson and later Trevor Hunter. Subsequently, she taught traditional fiddle and traditional piano back-up all her adult life. She started composing in her late 20's and has had two books published with a third on the way. Margaret's early musical influences were with her late father, Lell Robertson, either playing at home or listening to recordings. His enthusiasm for music never left him. As the Musical Director for Hjaltibonhoga, the Shetland Fiddlers of the Royal Edinburgh Military Tattoo, Margaret feels privileged to have brought traditional music to international stages in Scotland, Australia, New Zealand, Germany, Norway and China. In 2018, Margaret was inducted to the 'Hands up for Trad' Hall of Fame for services to the Community and was awarded the MBE in the 2020 Queen's Birthday Honours list for Services to Scottish Music. Throughout her career she has been fortunate to play music with many talented people and now, having moved to the Scottish Mainland, her musical opportunities are starting a new chapter.

 Catherine Robson was born and raised in Newcastle and had an interest in music from an early age, playing flute and piano. After an unhappy experience studying music at university, she decided never to have anything to do with music ever again! Until, that is, she discovered the world of folk music, initially the Northumbrian tradition. Catherine took up the Northumbrian smallpipes, attending classes at Newcastle University and then playing with Robson's Choice, a group of pipers and other musicians who fund-raise for a local hospice. She started writing the occasional tune for the smallpipes in 2000 but really got into tune-writing when chronic fatigue syndrome struck bringing a combination of severe insomnia and a need for a creative outlet. Since then, she has published two tune books, which are available via **www.robsonschoice.co.uk**, with all proceeds to St Oswald's Hospice.

 Alison Rowley is a musician, music teacher and composer based in Bristol. She performs in several professional ceilidh bands as a fiddle player and caller, teaches violin, fiddle and piano, and leads workshops in folk music and dance. In 2013 she was a Creative Artist In Residence at Cecil Sharp House, London, commissioned to write an orchestral fantasia of Cotswold Morris tunes. She has a Music degree from the University of Cambridge.
www.alisonrowley.com

 Olivia Ross is a fiddle player, singer and string instructor from the Highlands of Scotland where she still lives and works, as well as being a founder member of The Shee.

 Kerry Russell is a traditional fiddle player, who also gets to work in the Health Service. She has lived, worked and played with many wonderful people in a number of amazing places around the world. Now based in Dublin, with the Cobblestone as her local, she writes tunes to capture memories, ideas and emotions.

Laura-Beth Salter is a Lincolnshire-born, Glasgow based mandolinist, singer and composer and can be heard performing with award winning folk bands The Shee and Kinnaris Quintet, in a duo with Jenn Butterworth and 'From the Ground', a project with Ali Hutton. She was nominated for the MG Alba Composer of the Year award in 2013 after the success of her Celtic Connections commission and debut album *Breathe*. Laura-Beth is an active tutor of mandolin and youth projects all over the UK.

laurabethsalter.com

 Patsy Seddon from Edinburgh, is known for her clàrsach/Scottish harp playing and singing over many years with the duo Sileas, the group The Poozies and other ensembles including Clan Alba. With these line-ups she has performed numerous concerts over forty years and has recorded many albums. Traditional Scottish and Gaelic music is her first love, and she also composes tunes in traditional style. Patsy is an active teacher including Kodály musicianship for NYCoS (National Youth Choir of Scotland) and formerly at the Gaelic medium primary school Taobh na Pairce in Edinburgh. She has an honours degree in Celtic Studies and was one of the first musicians in residence at the School of Scottish Studies at Edinburgh University. She is currently Artistic Adviser for the Edinburgh International Harp Festival. In 2013, Patsy was inducted into the Scottish Traditional Music Hall of Fame for her part in the development of the Scottish Harp.

www.patsyseddon.com

 Grace Smith is a fiddle and viola player, and creates new folk music inspired by traditional archive material. She formed the Grace Smith Trio and is a member of the French dance band Cri du Canard. Grace is a dedicated music educator, having taught for organisations including National Youth Folk Ensemble, North East Fiddle School, Folkworks, Newcastle University, Band on the Wall, and Liverpool Philharmonic Youth Company.

www.gracesmithmusic.co.uk

 Eilidh Steel is a Scottish fiddler and composer from Helensburgh on the West Coast of Scotland. She started playing at the age of six and grew up immersed in both traditional and classical music, touring abroad with bands from the age of 16. Since graduating from the Royal Conservatoire of Scotland in Glasgow where she studied Scottish music, Eilidh has carved out an impressive career for herself as a performer, composer and tutor. She has always had a great interest in the West Highland fiddle tradition and a particular interest in music from her local area which she continues to research. Her self-published book 'West Highland Tunes for Beginner Fiddlers' quickly became a valuable resource for tutors, organisations and learners. She tours and records in a duo with guitarist and singer-songwriter Mark Neal, and performs with various other collaborations. Eilidh is also in great demand as a tutor at festivals and for various organisations throughout the UK and abroad.

www.eilidhsteel.com

 Anna-Wendy Stevenson is the third generation in the Stevenson family line of composer/performers. Her fiddling has been honed through years of playing with an array of Scotland's musicians including the legendary Jock Tamson's Bairns, pianist James Ross and the Simon Bradley Trio. She has produced several albums and recorded on many, collaborating with artists including her late grandfather, the composer pianist Ronald Stevenson on *Gowd and Silver*, the Simon Bradley Trio, the Far Flung Collective, James Ross, Fine Friday, Gillebride MacMillan, and Patsy Reid & Jim Sutherland's Commonwealth Games Commission 'Children of the Smoke'. Her own compositions include, 'My Edinburgh', a homage to her home city and 'Suite Uist' which was recorded with the Far Flung Collective, and has been performed in Canada, England and Scotland. Anna-Wendy is senior lecturer in music with the University of the Highlands and Islands and programme leader for the BA (Hons) Applied Music and recipient of several awards for her contribution to education including MG Alba Scots Trad Music Tutor of the Year 2018 and the Higher Education Academy Collaborative Award in Teaching Excellence 2021.

Wendy Stewart is a leading Scottish harper, a world class performer and inspirational teacher whose style and repertoire encompasses both traditional music and her own compositions. She has produced four solo recordings, several music books and teaches all level of student, from beginner to graduate, throughout Europe and the USA. These days much of Wendy's musical life and inspiration stems from her home range and community in bonny Glencairn. She continues to explore musical connections with the natural world, the spoken word, dance and science. Her most recent CD, *Folds in the Field*, is of her own music, inspired by Scotland's South West, and Wendy is a happy member of a local group, The Galloway Agreement.

www.cairnwatermusic.com

 Kate Strudwick lives in the South East Wales valleys and is a founder member of Welsh band Allan yn y Fan, combining this with her day job as Creative Director of community arts organisation Head4Arts. Kate was born in Wales to English parents but brought up elsewhere. Her love of traditional music was kindled by the BBC's *Singing Together* radio programme, then by visits to the Deer Leap Folk Club in Exmouth and Sidmouth Folk Festival. Since returning to Wales, she has spent more than two decades playing whistles, flute and recorders with Allan yn y Fan at concerts, festivals and twmpaths, both at home and abroad. With a continuous "soundtrack" in her head, Kate is a great supporter of "the living tradition" and the practice of capturing people, places and events in musical form, some of which have been included in the band's six CDs. She also loves encouraging people of all ages to learn more about traditional music, helping to set up new tune clubs across the area so they can share the pleasure of playing together.

www.ayyf.co.uk

 Vicki Swan is best known for playing in the folk duo Vicki Swan & Jonny Dyer and for teaching the nyckelharpa to as many people as possible at workshops around the country and the world on Zoom. Vicki studied at the Royal College of Music on the double bass, and also plays various types of bagpipes, flute, recorder, piano and nyckelharpa (Swedish keyed-fiddle). On leaving music college, Vicki started down the long path of folk music and was only seen on rare glimpses back in classical orchestras. You'll find her now inhabiting the troll ridden forests playing her nyckelharpa, bagging new tunes from the näcken – the magical water sprite known for giving up tunes to those travellers hardy enough to ask for them. Vicki has written countless tunes for all her instruments, it would be hard to count them all up as sometimes they run away under the sofa and refuse to come out. In the end most of the tunes are rounded up and end up on Vicki's Virtual Music Room teaching website.

www.swan-dyer.co.uk / www.nyckelharpa.me.uk

 Laurel Swift is a musician and composer, an inspiring instigator of creative new projects and performances rooted in the folk arts. She plays double bass and clog dances with Gadarene and plays fiddle with The Gloworms and in a duo with Ben Moss. Laurel is currently absorbed in 'Travelling with Thomas', a project to write a folk musical in public, inviting people to come on the journey and see inside the artistic process! She co-created and performed 'Under her Skin' with Debs Newbold. Laurel loves to dance and has choreographed for theatre and film and directed national touring dance productions for Morris Offspring. She also teaches folk music, with particular focus on helping people find their own ownership of our shared traditions through creative approaches to variation, ensemble skills and simply having a good time!

www.laurelswift.co.uk

Amy Thatcher is a professional accordionist based in North East England. She writes and performs with The Shee, Monster Ceilidh Band, with Kathryn Tickell, as a soloist and in a duo with Fran Knowles.

www.amythatcher.co.uk

 Inge Thomson is a multi-instrumentalist, composer and performer from Fair Isle (Shetland). Recently, she has been creating large scale multi-arts productions, film soundtrack/radio drama content, producing for other artists and regularly touring with the Karine Polwart Trio. She also performs and records in solo capacity and in cross-disciplinary collaborations including projects with scientists, visual artists, animators, theatre makers and textile artists.

 Kathryn Tickell is a Northumbrian piper, fiddle player and composer whose music is inspired by the landscape and people of Northumberland. In 2009, she was presented with The Queen's Medal for Music, awarded to those deemed to have made an outstanding contribution to British music and she was awarded an OBE in 2015. She has released many albums and has collaborated across many genres with musicians such as Sting, Evelyn Glennie, Andy Sheppard, Penguin Café Orchestra, Royal Northern Sinfonia and The Chieftains.

www.kathryntickell.com

 Karen Tweed lives in inspirational Orkney and is respected internationally as a multi-faceted artist, teacher and creative. Born in London in 1963, Karen took up the accordion at age 11; then studied Graphic Design (Printmaking) at Leeds before making music her career. Karen appears on over 70 CDs and produces her own videos and publications. She founded the No.1 Ladies Accordion Orchestra, May Monday (with Finnish composer/pianist Timo Alakotila) and the 21-strong female ensemble Circa Compania. A brilliant collaborator, she's worked with Kathryn Tickell, Karen Street, Ian Carr and Andy Cutting; she was a founder member of The Poozies, SWÅP and was the music director for Parrabbola Theatre Company's 'Land of Liberty'. In 2021 Karen was commissioned by Siamsa Tíre, the National Folk Theatre of Ireland and St Magnus Festival in Orkney.

www.karentweed.com

 Tina Jordan Rees is a Glasgow-based traditional musician originally from Lancashire. She is a multi-instrumentalist playing piano, flute and whistles, and is also a qualified Irish dance teacher. As an avid composer, Tina takes her influences from many places, including the Irish dance music tradition, where she is a household name.

www.tinajordanrees.com

 Branwen Mai Roberts is 9 years old and from Ystradgynlais where she lives by the river Tawe. She is beginning to learn how to play the Welsh bagpipes and her favourite type of music is Welsh folk tunes. Branwen is also learning how to play a lot of varied instruments including the harp and violin, and also hopes to start learning the cello. She loves reading, and prefers reading novels, with her favourite author being David Walliams. She also likes playing music and making craft. In her spare time she likes swimming and playing hockey. Branwen says, "I like living in Ystradgynlais because it is nice to be able to wake up in the morning and walk to the window, open the curtains and look on the river Tawe below."

Róisín Ward Morrow is a fiddle player, folk singer, and tune composer hailing from Co. Louth on Ireland's Ancient East. Her debut album, *By The Light of The Moon*, an album of slow airs, was released in 2019. Róisín's music is heart-led and inspired by inner healing, landscapes, and stories. Róisín is also the proud recipient of the Droichead Arts Bursary 2021, for 'Women of Folk Song' where she is researching and interpreting folk songs about the stories of women. She has performed extensively in venues around Ireland as well as touring internationally in the Netherlands and in The White House for President Obama. Róisin also featured on RTÉ, performing in 'Celebrate St. Patrick' recorded in St. Patrick's Cathedral, Armagh.

 Margaret Watchorn grew up in Northumberland amid a rich local and family heritage of music, dances, songs and stories, many learnt from her parents and grandparents. As a teenager in the 1970s, her father made her a set of Northumbrian smallpipes and she began playing at the Alnwick Pipers' Society, learning with Joe Hutton. After studying music at York University, Margaret returned to Northumberland to pursue a career in education, initially as a successful primary headteacher, then working with music from ages 0 to 18 – from singing with babies to teaching A level students. Most of all, she spent endless happy hours playing the fiddle and piano with musicians from the older generation. These days, Margaret performs regularly with her husband, Andy, a fine Northumbrian smallpipes player; they have strong links with musicians in Dalsland, Sweden and enjoy getting to grips with Swedish bagpipes (Andy) and nyckelharpa (Margaret). As well as directing an early music singing group and singing in a chamber choir, Margaret finds time for composing and for researching the music of north Northumberland.

 Rona Wilkie is a fiddle player and Gaelic singer, who has performed and recorded extensively in Scotland and across Europe over the last decade. As a composer, she has been commissioned to write several film scores, including for the BBC and for the BAFTA Best Picture Nominee *16 Years Till Summer*. She is also regularly invited to compose new commissions for festivals, including Celtic Connections, the Hippodrome Silent Film Festival and the Cantilena Festival. Rona has recently become more involved with songwriting, with a particular focus on considering minority-cultural identity. She has written with seven minority language composers in the European City of Culture funded project 'Tosta', and participated in the first minority language residency Mamiaith in Wales. Her most recent composition project, 'Gasta', re-examines the lives of young Gaels in Scotland and Ireland. Here she has collaborated closely with Irish-language songwriter Ríona Sally Hartman and Cian Mac Cárthaigh (of Imlé), alongside her long-time musical partner Marit Fält and Ross Whyte (of Whyte).

www.maritandrona.co.uk

 Heather Woodbridge grew up in the island of North Ronaldsay, the most northerly island in Orkney. She began the fiddle in primary school, through free one-to-one instrument tuition (offered to all school students in Orkney since 1973) and also plays the piano. Orkney has strong connections with Norway, and Heather was offered a student exchange scholarship for a year's study in Hordaland (now Vestland). She studied Musikk at Voss Folkehøgskule, taking lessons on the Hardanger fiddle with the late, Leif Rygg. She was the last Orkney student to enjoy this exchange as funding ran out. In 2013, Heather went on to study Ecology at the University of Stirling, graduating with a First Class Honours degree in 2017. She worked in conservation and informal musical tuition then settled back home in Orkney. Following her father Kevin Woodbridge's unexpected passing in April 2020, she stood for his vacant seat in a Council by-election and was elected in October 2020. First elected at the age of 26, Heather was (until 2022) the youngest ever elected member to sit on Orkney Islands Council, and still is the youngest ever woman. She is now Deputy Leader of the Council.

Karen Woods (née Logan) hails from County Antrim in Northern Ireland and, having been an Irish dancer as a child, started playing traditional Irish music in her late teens. She plays wooden flute, whistles, fiddle and bodhrán. Her repertoire is mostly Irish, with a good few Scottish and English tunes, as well as music from other world traditions. Over the years Karen has composed many traditional style tunes and is currently self employed as a ceilidh musician and caller, DJ and dance facilitator. She plays in 'Trad' music sessions around Bristol and Bath, most regularly in 'The Star' in Bristol. Karen says, "Live music makes the world a better place, and playing traditional music adds such richness and beauty to life."

soundcloud.com/karenwoodsmusic/tracks

 Martha Woods is a fiddle player, guitarist, singer, and composer from Cornwall. Having grown up playing and dancing for traditional Cornish dance group Tan Ha Dowr and writing songs for her band, The Woodcarts, Martha discovered the joy of writing tunes while studying on the Folk and Traditional Music degree at Newcastle University and has continued with this while studying on a year abroad at the University of Limerick. While Martha draws inspiration for her compositions from the music of her home in Cornwall, she is influenced by many different traditional music styles of Britain, Ireland and America. She hopes to write playable and memorable tunes that everyone can enjoy!

FOLK TUNES FROM THE WOMEN

100 Days & Better Than a Bill
Copyright © 2023 Anna Massie

A Far Away Rebel & View from the Dam
Copyright © 2023 Adèle Commins

A Girl on the Rock & Lle Arall
Copyright © 2023 Kate Strudwick

A Quiet Autumn & Granny in the Attic
Copyright © 2023 Sarah Allen

A Tune for Frankie & The Red Crow
Copyright © 2023 Mairéad Ní Mhaonaigh

A Tune for Jean, Crow Road Croft
& Lady Isabella
Copyright © 2023 Lauren MacColl

A Tune for Lewis
Copyright © 2023 Kirstie McLanaghan

Against Time
Copyright © 2023 Éadaoin Ní Mhaicín

Akaroa
Copyright © 2023 Annette Davies

Alan Friendly, The Bass Strathspey
& The Phrayes
Copyright © 2023 Corrina Hewat

Alaw i Nansi
Copyright © 2023 Llio Rhydderch

Andy's Saltire & Rounding Malin Head
Copyright © 2023 Zoë Conway

Angus Grant Sings the Grateful Dead
& Otis & Deanie
Copyright © 2023 Sarah McFadyen

Anne et Ludovic, La Femme du Saule
& The Underwater Gardener
Copyright © 2023 Sarah Northcott

Another Day
Copyright © 2023 Karen Gledhill

April's Child, Emergency of the Female Kind
& Too Cute to Correct
Copyright © 2023 Amy Thatcher

Arthur's Seat, Fàilte & Nuala Iona's Jig
Copyright © 2023 Anna-Wendy Stevenson

Aye Fly & Flame
Copyright © 2023 Bryony Griffith

Back Home in Önsbacken &
The Lighthouse Lovers
Copyright © 2023 Karen Tweed

The Ballymena Polka, Ivan's &
Swerving for Bunnies
Copyright © 2023 Ailie Robertson

The Beachcomber & Maisie's Jig
Copyright © 2023 Kerry Russell

Bealaclare Bridge & New Year's Resolutions
Copyright © 2023 Mairéad Carey

Beccy's Big day & Knoydart Ahoy!
Copyright © 2023 Olivia Ross

Bert Mackenzie's 70th Birthday Waltz
Copyright © 2023 Louise Mackenzie

The Bird Man of Chambers Street,
Laidback Liz & Pipe Major Bobby Coghill of Wick
Copyright © 2023 Eilidh Steel

Bonfire Night & Good News for Pigs
Copyright © 2023 Helen Gentile

Bresychen Ddiog
Copyright © 2023 Elsa Davies

Bright Field
Copyright © 2023 Rowan Rheingans

Byddwch Yn Garedig
Copyright © 2023 Mari Morgan

The Caledon Line & Grey Days
Copyright © 2023 Chloë Bryce

The Calm Between the Storms,
Paw Bran & Spring At last
Copyright © 2023 Martha Woods

Castle Hill & Rosa's Waltz
Copyright © 2023 Delyth Jenkins

Chin Up
Copyright © 2023 Rachel Cross

The Christmas Eve Waltz &
Sheila & Gordon's Golden Wedding March
Copyright © 2023 Marie Fielding

Cissy Middleton of Gawthrop
Copyright © 2023 Carolyn Francis

Claggy Jacks & Marram
Copyright © 2023 Margaret Watchorn

Clogfaenydd
Copyright © 2023 Bethan Rhiannon

Da Fiddler Fae Soothower, Linda's Lilt &
Michael's Birthday Jig
Copyright © 2023 Margaret Robertson

The Dale & Parmogeddon
Copyright © 2023 Grace Smith

Dark Stacks
Copyright © 2023 Inge Thomson

Dawns Elmo
Copyright © 2023 Cerys Hafana

Deoraíocht an t-Saighdiúra, Rhubarb and Ginger
& The Two-Part Pour Polka
Copyright © 2023 Niamh Ní Charra

The Devil's Schottis & The Halsway Parade
Copyright © 2023 Vicki Swan

'Dolig Abertawe, Key Workers Waltz & Y Selar
Copyright © 2023 Angharad Jenkins

Don MacDonald & Wilbur's Wonder
Copyright © 2023 Sue Harris

Don't Work Too Hard & Yer Peaks Are
Getting Peakier
Copyright © 2023 Laura-Beth Salter

Dram Behind the Curtain, The First Rule of Box
Club & Maggie West's Waltz
Copyright © 2023 Mairearad Green

Ducks at Luss & Tripod's Frolics
Copyright © 2023 Tina Jordan Rees

Dusseldram
Copyright © 2023 Cathy Geldard

The East Clare Jig & The Legacy
Copyright © 2023 Cliodhna Donnellan

The Eggshell Brewery, Loch nan Claidheamhan
& Up the Lum
Copyright © 2023 Rachel Newton

Elvaston Castle, Holtwood Reel & Mr Collins' No. 2
Copyright © 2023 Jess Arrowsmith

For Marie & Mike & Catherine's
Copyright © 2023 Isla Callister

Four for a Boy, Hunter's Path
& Selkie's Echo
Copyright © 2023 Alison Jones

Freya Dances & The Trip to Gorthleck
Copyright © 2023 Mary Macmaster

Gen-Z
Copyright © 2023 Imogen Bose-Ward

George Veness 2, Swirling Flames & Tanteeka
Copyright © 2023 Jo Freya

The Great Exodus & Sandy MacDonald of Skye
Copyright © 2023 Gráinne Brady

Haul ar y Carreg
Copyright © 2023 Stacey Blythe

I Fear You Just as I Fear Ghosts &
Welcome Joy and Welcome Sorrow
By Jane Harbour
Copyright © 2009 & 2015 Real World Works

Jiggin' in Meitheal
Copyright © 2023 Ernestine Healy

Jamie's Jig & Johnnie Armstrong
Copyright © 2023 Patsy Seddon

John MacDougall's March
Copyright © 2023 Amy Geddes

Jolly Roger & Time for a Jig
Copyright © 2023 Pam Bishop

The Joy of It! & Tune for A.Lien
Copyright © 2023 Catriona Macdonald

Kilmartin Glen Campsite & Tha i air sràid
Copyright © 2023 Rona Wilkie

King Bramble & Season's Promise
Copyright © 2023 Laurel Swift

Kingfisher on the Clun
Copyright © 2023 Ruth Angell

Lament for Emily Davison &
Tweedmouth Hornpipe
Copyright © 2023 Susie Cochrane

Last Trip to Dunbar
Copyright © 2023 Catherine Robson

Learn to Hambo!, Maddie's Mayhem
& Paperwork Sucks
Copyright © 2023 Sophy Ball

Leaving Whitby & Pillowfish
Copyright © 2023 Helen Bell

Llidiart y mynydd
Copyright © 2023 Gwen Màiri

The Lockdown Polka
Copyright © 2023 Maeve McCann

Longshaw's
Copyright © 2023 Alison Rowley

Lurand
Copyright © 2023 Heather Woodbridge

Mae'r Gaeaf yn Dyfod
Copyright © 2023 Branwen Mai Roberts

May the Road Rise Up to Meet You
& Moniaive Jig
Copyright © 2023 Wendy Stewart

Mazurka
Copyright © 2023 Catrin Ashton

Mazurka in the Dark & Puck Goes Dancing
Copyright © 2023 Harriet Power

Mirain
Copyright © 2023 Helina Rees

Morag's Welcome & Society's Welcome
to the Year '21
Copyright © 2023 Claire Gullan

Mynydd Du
Copyright © 2023 Lucy Rivers

Neuketyneuks & Suilven
Copyright © 2023 Fiona Driver

Never Trust Google Maps & Revoke Article 50
Copyright © 2023 Isla Ratcliff

Old Wax Jacket
Copyright © 2023 Tamsin Elliott

Pandemonium
Copyright © 2023 Rebecca McCarthy-Kent

The Pinnacle & Stretching Heart
Copyright © 2023 Christine Edwards

The Port Dash
Copyright © 2023 Róisín Ward Morrow

Rede River Girls, Rothbury Road
& The Welcome Home
Copyright © 2023 Kathryn Tickell

The Rest and be Thankful
Copyright © 2023 Marit Fält

Rita Hunter of Aultbea
Copyright © 2023 Valerie Bryan

Seren yn y Glascoed
Copyright © 2023 Angharad Jones

The Shores of Loch Awe
Copyright © 2023 Karen Woods

The Sliding Rocks & Tilly Trip
Copyright © 2023 Breesha Maddrell

Springa Like Marit & Thugainn
Copyright © 2023 Patsy Reid

Steve Fisher's Lament
Copyright © 2023 Mel Biggs

Traeth y Bermo
Copyright © 2023 Mirain Owen

Trip to Bucharest & Waltzing at Giggleswick
Copyright © 2023 Rachael McShane

Uncle Alan's Curtsy
Copyright © 2023 Marina Dodgson